"If you tend to put things off, *A Teen's Guide to Getting Stuff Done* will help you to understand the reasons for your procrastination and (more importantly) what you can do about it. It's filled with commonsense, step-by-step tools that will help you to break the cycle of stalling and start getting things done. So, don't delay—check out this book now!"

> —**Martin M. Antony, PhD, ABPP**, professor of psychology at Ryerson University in Toronto, ON, Canada, and coauthor of *The Shyness and Social Anxiety Workbook*

"It's not often you hear about procrastination without judgment or shame. Jennifer Shannon takes a compassionate approach to the complexities of why people procrastinate, and what can be done about it. Although this guide is for teens, I suggest anyone who suffers from the disappointment that can come with not completing a task read this, as well. As a temperament specialist, I appreciate the invitation for teens to understand their procrastination style and type, such as the perfectionist, the warrior, the pleaser, and the rebel. This book is right on target, and is bound to lead to less stress and more success!"

> —**Rona Renner, RN**, parenting coach and author of
> *Is That Me Yelling?*

"The Shannons have done it again! Like their other books, *A Teen's Guide to Getting Stuff Done* is engaging, easy to understand, and graphically entertaining. Teens and older readers alike will enjoy figuring out their procrastination type and discovering skills to conquer it. Reading this book is one step procrastinators will find both doable and rewarding. Enjoy the ride!"

—**Christine A. Padesky, PhD**, coauthor of *Mind Over Mood*

"Jennifer Shannon's newest book is an outstanding resource for getting out of your own way when it comes to procrastination. I will be gifting every one of my parenting friends a copy of *A Teen's Guide to Getting Stuff Done*. Thank you, Jennifer, for another great resource!"

—**Sharon L. Bowman, MA**, author of *Training from the BACK of the Room!* and *Using Brain Science to Make Training Stick*

"*A Teen's Guide to Getting Stuff Done* is incredibly readable, and most of all—useful! Shannon clearly knows her audience and the daily challenges that are in our way. Her examples are vividly real, and her solutions are all about ultimate freedom from our inner obstacles."

—**Ellie Dwight**, assistant head of school at Sonoma Academy in Santa Rosa, CA

the *i*nstant help
solutions series

Young people today need mental health resources more than ever. That's why New Harbinger created the **Instant Help Solutions Series** especially for teens. Written by leading psychologists, physicians, and professionals, these evidence-based self-help books offer practical tips and strategies for dealing with a variety of mental health issues and life challenges teens face, such as depression, anxiety, bullying, eating disorders, trauma, and self-esteem problems.

Studies have shown that young people who learn healthy coping skills early on are better able to navigate problems later in life. Engaging and easy-to-use, these books provide teens with the tools they need to thrive—at home, at school, and on into adulthood.

This series is part of the **New Harbinger Instant Help Books** imprint, founded by renowned child psychologist Lawrence Shapiro. For a complete list of books in this series, visit newharbinger.com.

a teen's guide* to getting stuff done

discover your procrastination type, stop putting things off & reach your goals

JENNIFER SHANNON, LMFT
ILLUSTRATIONS BY DOUG SHANNON

Instant Help Books
An Imprint of New Harbinger Publications, Inc.

Publisher's Note

Distributed in Canada by Raincoast Books

Copyright © 2017 by Jennifer Shannon
        Instant Help Books
        An Imprint of New Harbinger Publications, Inc.
        5674 Shattuck Avenue
        Oakland, CA 94609
        www.newharbinger.com

Illustrations by Doug Shannon; Cover design by Amy Shoup; Acquired by Tesilya Hanauer; Edited by Karen Schader

Library of Congress Cataloging-in-Publication Data on file

Printed in the United States of America

19   18   17

10   9   8   7   6   5   4   3   2   1   First printing

Contents

Chapter 1

Procrastination: Problem or Solution?

If you consider yourself a procrastinator, you're in good company. Whether it's making a difficult phone call or decision, doing homework or working out, getting out of bed in the morning or into bed at night, we all put things off at times. And that's not always a bad thing.

Leaving a difficult task to the last minute can create a sense of urgency that helps you focus on it. When you ignore a problem, it may take care of itself, and sometimes the thing you didn't get done is something you didn't truly want to do in the first place. But as many of us have experienced, when we regularly postpone tasks and obligations that we want or need to do, we pay a price.

The price is usually paid in self-esteem. Chronic procrastinators don't feel happy and proud about it. If you're a procrastinator, you have likely been told that you are lazy, disorganized, unmotivated, maybe even stupid. People who don't have this problem can be very judgmental. It can feel like they are being mean, but they are most likely worried about you. They want you to succeed, and they can see how procrastination could be getting in the way of your success. They too may have problems with procrastination and share the burden of shame. They don't want you to suffer as they have. But their comments, no matter how well intentioned, usually make matters worse. *@ Mom + Dad*

When we hear negative judgments about ourselves often enough, we tend to internalize them. You may be beating yourself up for your lack of motivation or

The price we pay for procrastination is usually diminished self-esteem.

organization, or your inability to get things done. You ask yourself, *Why do I put off tasks I know I have to do, and sometimes even want to do? Why can't I make myself do what's necessary to get where I want to go?* Unable to answer these questions, you can easily get discouraged. Without compassion for yourself, procrastination is hard to live with.

From my experience working with both teens and adults, I can say with authority that putting things off doesn't mean you are bad, lazy, stupid, or in any other way inferior.

Thank you!!!

Procrastination is not a sign of weakness or moral failing. It's simply a human problem. And the challenge is bigger for you ← than it was for your parents. [Our smartphones and computers are increasingly powerful agents of distraction that make staying focused on tasks more difficult every day. Wherever you are, distraction is only a click away. Social media, email, and text messages beckon night and day. If you don't respond immediately, you might hurt someone's feelings or miss out on something cool. No previous generation had to deal with the powerful distractions of the digital age.] *AMEN!*

Much of the help and advice given to procrastinators is about how you can organize yourself to meet deadlines, with lots of rules to follow. Time management is indeed important; I have a whole chapter devoted to it later in the book. However, to solve your procrastination problem at the core, it's more important to understand the person who is managing that time—you.

Procrastination is not a sign of weakness or moral failing.

Your sensibility, your temperament, your values and motivations do not fit neatly into a one-size-fits-all definition of the procrastinator. Neither you nor the problem of procrastination is that simple. To better identify how procrastination works with you, I have divided those of us with a tendency to put things off into four types, each with its own values, weaknesses, and strengths, as well as reasons for procrastinating.

Are you the perfectionist, who has to get things right; the warrior, who must feel fully engaged; the pleaser, who must keep everyone happy; or the rebel, who resists doing what others ask or assign? Don't be too quick to answer. There's a little of each type in all of us.

Whether you are one pure type or a hybrid of two or more, you'll want to know more about them all. In the next few chapters we'll explore the worlds of the perfectionist, the warrior, the pleaser, and the rebel, discovering the unique vulnerability of each to procrastination, as well as the hidden superpower each can tap into to master challenging tasks.

If you want to improve your ability to get things done—not to please your parents, teachers, and friends, but to better meet your personal goals in life—this book is for you. I'll show you how to master not only your to-dos, but also your life!

[handwritten marginalia: one of the reasons]

Chapter 2

The Perfectionist

Imagine a class of high school seniors on a field trip to Paris. Their teacher, Madam Fontaine, has a list of the landmarks she wants her students to visit; however, they have only one day in the city to see them all. To help motivate them, she sets up a competition, a kind of scavenger hunt. She divides her class randomly—or so she thinks—into four teams and announces that whichever team returns to the hotel by sundown having witnessed all the landmarks on the list will have that night's curfew extended by two hours. Bidding them adieu, she sets them loose.

Team #1 decides that they should have a solid plan in place, so they order coffee and scones at a café and huddle over the list. There is much discussion over the best sequence.

Should they begin with the closest attraction or get the farthest one out of the way? When lunchtime rolls around, they're still debating. Every time a plan is made, it is second-guessed and discarded. When the café closes, they realize the day is half gone, and in desperation they pool their funds for an Uber. After much high-speed maneuvering through traffic, they manage to check off only three attractions before getting stuck in rush hour. They wind up watching the sun set behind the Arc de Triomphe, miles away from their hotel and the prize.

This team is made up of *Perfectionists*. When perfectionists are 100 percent confident that they know exactly how they're going to accomplish a task successfully, they have no trouble getting started. But if there's any chance that they aren't prepared or might make a mistake, perfectionists will delay. Only when the deadline is so near that time will not allow perfection will the perfectionist do the task. For the perfectionist, the only thing that will override the fear of getting it wrong is the fear of not getting it done at all.

Jordan

Jordan is a high school sophomore and a classic perfectionist. (Like all the characters in this book, Jordan is not an actual person, but rather a composite of teens I've seen in my practice.) He's driven and gets good grades, but boy does he suffer. Ever since middle school, when he started to think more about his future, Jordan began to worry more about his grades. In Jordan's mind, if he doesn't get into a good college, he won't be successful in life.

He's not wrong in some ways ←

Jordan will do research and draft outlines for a paper but then agonize about how to get started. He'll obsess over whether he picked the right topic, whether he did enough research, and how he will be graded. He often doesn't get around to writing the first sentence until the night before the paper is due. Often he's unable to finish in time and will beg his mother to write an excuse so he can skip school the next day.

The worry and stress Jordan creates for himself takes a toll. He feels guilty about not starting sooner and when he sees his classmates' progress, he feels panic rise within him. Staying up all night to complete projects that he has put off makes him tired and irritable the next day. Worst of all, his procrastination is hurting his grades.

If you suggested to Jordan that he was a perfectionist, he'd laugh. *No way*, he'd say. *I'm always messing up! If I were perfect, I wouldn't be procrastinating!*

But being a perfectionist doesn't mean you're perfect. It means you believe you should be. Jordan believes that he should know what he's going to say, say it clearly, and not struggle with the concepts. If he does find himself struggling, he thinks something must be wrong, and he needs to stop and

honestly, me too ←

figure it out so that he can correct it. As long as he remains uncertain, he puts the task off.

Working with these restrictions, Jordan is always hedging his bets, embracing only the activities and projects he can excel at. Instead of feeling motivated by his passion for excellence, he's limited by his fear of failure. Although he wants to succeed and be happy in life, what drives him is fear of being "less than." If Jordan loses his position at the top of his class, he'll feel like a failure. What would others think of him if he didn't get into a top college? He could lose the respect of his parents, his teachers, even his friends!

The core value of the perfectionist is excellence.

You don't need to be aiming for an exclusive college to be a perfectionist. Needing to excel at anything—sports, music, fashion, business, even popularity—to feel respected qualifies. If you procrastinate because you worry about making mistakes, you're a perfectionist.

★ This is why I think I
procrastinated over working out ★

I'm definitely a little "perfectionist"

Making decisions can be a constant problem for the perfectionist, who always believes there is only one correct choice. Whether you're buying a pair of shoes or deciding on a college, you always need more time. When you can't be sure you're right, you're paralyzed, unable to commit to any choice at all. To others, this can look like laziness or lack of motivation, but the perfectionist isn't lazy. You're working overtime, agonizing over making the correct choice.

Even low-stakes situations can be a challenge when perfectionists apply their high standards to them. You may only need to write a thank-you note, but if you think the note must sound flawlessly sincere, you can be immobilized and wind up writing nothing at all. And of course, the hurt feelings at the other end would be exactly the opposite of what you were after.

The perfectionist may also hesitate at initiating social interactions, like inviting people to do things. When you believe you always need to sound smart, interesting, and funny, and never be rejected, you'll put off reaching out to others. You may want to have more friends, yet you choose to stay home alone.

As a perfectionist who takes up a hobby, like playing a musical instrument or a sport, you may put off practicing it. Learning new things involves making mistakes, which the perfectionist cannot tolerate. Although you love the guitar, and you may even have loads of natural talent, you eventually give it up. Your need to be excellent keeps you from developing the excellence you seek.

While the perfectionist has the highest standard—excellence—your need to meet that standard makes meeting it impossible. Tasks that you aren't sure you can do perfectly must be avoided. You would risk being discovered as "less than" or "not good enough," and losing the respect of others. That's a risk the perfectionist is unable to take.

Are you a perfectionist? Here are ten statements for you to test on yourself. If you identify with five or more of them, perfectionism contributes to your procrastination. You can download the *Am I a Perfectionist?* quiz at http://www .newharbinger.com/35876. Later in the book, you'll find other quizzes and worksheets that can be downloaded; at the back of the book, you'll find information on how to access these downloadable materials.

I often procrastinate on tasks where others may judge my performance.

If a task is more difficult or frustrating than I expected, I often give up.

I often put challenging tasks off until I am clearheaded and confident I can do a good job.

I worry that others will lose respect for me or think I am incompetent if I make a mistake or am not the best at something.

I get upset when I make a mistake.

I don't like to start something if I don't feel certain I can do it well.

If someone does something better than I do, it makes me feel inferior.

√ *When I procrastinate, I feel guilty and tell myself I should get started.*

√ *I tend to get behind in my work because it takes me a long time to get things done right.*

√ *I criticize my own work so much that I don't feel like I've accomplished anything.*

The perfectionist's valuation of excellence can inspire you to the heights of achievement. On the other hand, your *need* to be excellent can be your greatest impediment to success. Fear of failing or being judged not good enough will not only get in the way of getting started but also keep you from being creative and taking risks, leaving you further away from "excellent" than ever. This is the dilemma of the perfectionist.

It's funny b/c I was convinced I wasn't anywhere near being a perfectionist

Chapter 3

The Warrior

Returning to our story, it is morning and Madam Fontaine
has just released her charges on a scavenger hunt of Parisian
attractions.

*Team #2 is hot off the mark, racing up the street, whooping
with enthusiasm. Within a half hour they are taking panorama
selfies from atop the Eiffel Tower. Soon after, their enthusiasm*

wanes a bit at the Louvre, and Notre Dame does not impress them. "What is this list," one member grumbles, "just a bunch of museums and churches?" When they happen to stumble across Le Geode, a huge geodesic dome with a mirrored finish and an IMAX theater inside, they perk up. "We've got all day," another suggests. "Why not see Jurassic Park 4 *in French first?" When they emerge from the theater, they have a shocking realization. "What! It's that late already?" Needless to say, they will not win the prize.*

These students are what I call *Warriors*. So long as warriors are fully engaged—running up the stairs of the Eiffel Tower, taking selfies at the top—they will embrace tasks with enthusiasm and focus. When a task fails to engage and boredom sets in, the warrior is easily distracted, often deciding, *There's plenty of time; I'll do it later.* Like a shark, the warrior must keep moving to stay alive, or at least, to *feel* alive.

Emily

Emily is a high school junior, an active person with a lot of energy. When Emily is rock climbing, dancing, or playing video games, she's fully engaged. But activities that aren't stimulating and challenging don't hold her attention, and she puts them off. As Emily describes herself, "I'm allergic to boredom." Her family and friends wouldn't disagree.

A great example was when Emily had the opportunity to go to Sweden for a year as an exchange student. She longed to travel, so she signed on without hesitation. It turned out that there was a lot more paperwork required than she expected.

Sitting still and answering questions thoughtfully was tedious for Emily, and every time she sat down to do it she got distracted. It was hard to focus when, for example, her friends were texting her to join in an online game, especially because she was the best player and they would lose without her. Although Emily made a heroic effort to pull everything together at the last minute, she couldn't get all her references in time and she missed the deadline.

The warrior is motivated by stimulation, opportunity, excitement; in one word, *engagement*. When you're in the zone, you get hyperfocused; the sense of time passing disappears and you can do amazing things. Unfortunately, that full engagement can make you lose track of everything else, causing you to literally forget about other tasks and deadlines. You think you have plenty of time to get things done and are continually surprised when the task you were putting off is due *now*!

Conversely, when the warrior is not fully engaged, time slows to a painful crawl, making you easily susceptible to distractions. Routine obligations like cleaning your room, getting ready for school, or doing homework feel like impossible tasks, as if you were trying to run underwater. You may like the idea of having all your homework done and being prepared for tests, but you don't feel motivated enough

definitely a little bit of "warrior"

yes ma'am

yep!

to get started on it. Once you finally get around to studying or writing, you may even get into it, feeling satisfaction in getting it done, and pledging to stay on top of assignments in the future. But due to the warrior's distorted experience of time, daily planning is especially difficult.

Even getting ready for dates or rides with friends can be a problem for the warrior. Absorbed in whatever you're doing in the moment, you'll put off getting ready until your friends are already at the door. People accuse you of being chronically late for everything, and you feel bad about that. But unless an activity is immediately engaging, it just doesn't feel important enough to be done right away and it's easily forgotten.

It's not that you're trying to frustrate others. You're late for your own obligations to yourself, too. You may have every intention of going out for a run or hike, but thinking there's plenty of time, you end up watching movies on your computer until your parents announce it's time to go to your grandparents' house for dinner (which you'd forgotten about) and you don't have time for your run.

In the quest for excitement and challenge, warriors know no bounds. You've got big dreams of winning, traveling, hobbies, or elaborate exercise programs, and you'll often start with a bang. But when you encounter the tedious steps that are necessary to move forward, you begin to lose steam and put off what you had begun.

The most reliable motivator for the warrior is the pressure of an imminent deadline. When something absolutely must be done immediately and quickly, the warrior can feel engaged even with boring tasks. Somehow you do your best thinking at midnight the day the paper is due. You'll ignore the engine light on your dashboard for weeks, but when the car stalls on

Today w/ Maggie + the wood

Explains me perfectly!

the freeway you'll jump into action. For the warrior, the best time to write a thank-you note for a birthday gift is a week before your *next* birthday. And the most engaging time to make a big meal for yourself is after you've gone all day so absorbed in something that you've forgotten to eat and are suddenly famished.

The other thing that can motivate you is your parents' or friends' nagging. Doing what they want is the only way to get them to stop. But this doesn't leave them, or you, feeling very good about what you've accomplished.

Not really, but okay

How do you engage in tasks when there's no immediate deadline and nobody nagging you? You may want a job so you can earn money and

The core value of the warrior is engagement.

may even enjoy searching for different jobs in your area, but downloading and filling out job applications feels tedious. You're filling out the online application, but then there's a social media notification and the next thing you know, you've forgotten about applying to that job, and the position is filled.

The tendency to move away from tasks that fail to engage you and toward distractions, combined with the time-management problems of the warrior, can create chaos in your life—low blood sugar-induced mood swings; poor grades; irritated parents, teachers, and friends. You may feel ashamed,

Yep!

disappointed, and frustrated. So you return to the stimulating activities you love, where warriors thrive, forgetting the tasks you need to get done to move your life forward.

How much of a warrior are you? Read the following ten statements to yourself. If five or more feel true, your warrior nature is contributing to your procrastination.

I have trouble staying organized, especially with schoolwork.

Sticking with things is difficult for me.

I have trouble concentrating on just one thing at a time.

I put things off because I don't feel like doing them.

I have trouble sticking with assignments I find boring.

It is easy for me to put assignments out of my mind and become distracted by other things.

There are many school assignments that I find boring and am not committed to or don't feel enthusiastic about.

I get restless easily and want to get up and move around.

I often start things but don't finish them.

It is hard to sit still for very long unless I am totally engrossed in what I am doing.

You can also download the *Am I a Warrior?* quiz at http://www.newharbinger.com/35876.

18

With a core value like full engagement, the warrior is capable of great things. Your high energy and ability to hyperfocus is like a superpower. But even Superman has his kryptonite, and for the warrior it is boredom and the misperception of time. When a task fails to engage the warrior, time seems to stop until a distraction brings relief. Tasks that need to get done for the warrior to advance to the next level—where you will not be bored—don't get done. The new challenges that will fully engage you are out of reach.

Chapter 4

The Pleaser

Back in Paris again, our story continues ...

Team #3 wastes no time getting started. Madam Fontaine is so enthusiastic about the hunt, and they want to make her happy. By noon they have checked off half the landmarks and are having loads of fun. Then they arrive at the famous neighborhood of Montmartre, where a street artist approaches one of them and offers to sketch a portrait. Not wanting to disappoint the artist, the student agrees. Another street vendor, peddling necklaces, calls out to the group, and because they all have difficulty saying "Non, merci," they feel obliged to look. Between the artists, the vendors, and the street mimes who grimace and shed invisible tears whenever the group tries to leave, they linger well into the afternoon. Only when the sun begins to disappear behind the tallest trees and buildings do they dash off in what will be a fruitless effort to complete the rest of the list.

This team represents a type of procrastinator that I call the *Pleaser*. Pleasers are so unwilling to risk making others unhappy—yes, sometimes even strangers—that they postpone their own needs to please them. Those who put their social connections above doing the tasks they themselves need to get done qualify as pleasers.

Athena

Athena is one of the nicest people you will ever meet. Her family refers to her, only half in jest, as "the good daughter." Athena has always found it easy to make friends; she has a boyfriend she's been dating since her freshman year and several girlfriends she's known since grade school. While those long-term relationships have given her a lot of pleasure and security, maintaining them sometimes comes at a cost.

A good example of this was the weekend of her family's mountain retreat, something Athena had been looking forward to for several months. They planned to get up early, make the four-hour drive, then hike an amazing trail before checking into their rented cabin. Athena bought a new camera just for the trip. She was planning on reading the manual, packing her clothes, and getting to bed early Friday night.

She was extra excited that her parents had promised to let her drive for part of the trip.

But when Athena's boyfriend called on Friday morning announcing that he had two tickets to see his favorite local band that evening, she couldn't bear to disappoint him. *He's so excited,* she thought. *I can pack and get ready this afternoon instead.*

Athena was just starting to pack when she got a text that stopped her short. Her girlfriends were on their way to the mall, and they insisted she join them. Athena didn't want to go to the mall any more than she wanted to go to the concert, but she knew how her girlfriends could be if she

refused—not mean exactly, just a little sharp and resentful. So she went to the mall with them before meeting her boyfriend.

Athena wound up packing at one in the morning, and she was too sleepy to drive the next day. Because she hadn't had time to review how her new camera worked, she didn't take any photos. Although she maintained an outwardly cheerful manner—she didn't want to disappoint her family—it wasn't a happy time for Athena.

Athena isn't so different from the rest of us. We all need to belong to family, friend, and social groups. But how badly do you need others to like you? When you sense that people may be displeased by something you do, do you feel anxious that they will be so upset that they may not like you anymore, or that you could be rejected or abandoned? When you feel this way, any activity or task where there is a risk of displeasing someone will feel threatening. You'll want to put it off if possible.

For example, if your sister asks to borrow something you don't want to lend, you'll avoid giving her an answer she doesn't want to hear. You'll also doubt yourself, wondering whether you're just being selfish. You believe that you cannot tell someone no unless you're certain you're 100 percent justified. Balancing others' needs with your own makes you doubtful and confused.

If you haven't called a friend in a long time, you may be hesitant to call even though you care about that person. Because you let so much time go by, you're now afraid your friend will be mad at you. The longer you put it off, the harder it is to reach out.

While the pleaser has opinions and preferences, you hesitate to express them when there's a chance that others may disagree with you. When planning things with friends, you get so overwhelmed thinking of what others will want to do that you don't know what you want. You feel responsible for other people's happiness and if they're disappointed, you'll be at fault. So you usually wait until others decide where to go, where to eat, or what movie to see.

When the pleaser has something that needs to get done, like studying, or getting your chores done, or looking for a job, you may put it off because you're too busy doing things for other people. If you sit down to study and a friend wants to text, you'll put off your studying rather than letting your friend down. This is standard behavior when you believe other people's needs are more important than your own. You often end up making elaborate excuses for why you didn't get something done, or lying about having done something you haven't, and later feeling terribly guilty about it.

The pleaser, whose core value is social connection, can only do what you are certain everyone will approve of. When others need or want your attention, your personal tasks are put aside for later. Focusing on your own agenda could disappoint them and threaten your connection. Other actions that we don't think of as tasks, like disagreeing with someone, telling an uncomfortable truth, or standing up for ourselves, can displease others too, and are put off as long as possible.

The core value of the pleaser is social connection.

Not sure if you're a pleaser? Read the following ten statements. If five or more feel true, you are definitely a pleaser, which contributes a lot to procrastination.

I tend to put others' needs before my own.

I feel guilty when I procrastinate and tell myself I should just do it.

When I feel uncertain about something, I put off making a decision.

I often agree to do things I don't really want to do and then put off getting them done.

It's hard for me to say no to someone.

I have things I should do that I don't feel committed to.

If I state an opinion or preference and others are upset by it, I feel responsible for making them feel bad.

I am more comfortable if others make decisions for me.

I often put off talking to someone if I know what I have to say might upset that person.

I don't like to disappoint people.

You can download the *Am I a Pleaser?* quiz at http://www .newharbinger.com/35876.

26

Nobody has a greater potential for deep friendship and intimacy than the pleaser, who values social connection above all else and is willing to work for it. But when your priority is making others happy, you aren't revealing your authentic self. Without authenticity, you continually miss out on the deep and honest connections you desire.

Chapter 5

The Rebel

Once again, we resume our story.

The last group of Madam Fontaine's students all agree on one thing. "This hunt is ridiculous! The Bastille isn't even on the list, and what could be cooler than a medieval prison?" They take off on their own, touring the grittier, less touristy parts of Paris. Late in the afternoon they strike up a conversation with some local teens, who offer to take them to see a great band that night. Remembering the prize of an extended curfew, which they will need to see the band, the team dashes off in a mad frenzy to complete the hunt. Alas, like the rest of Madam Fontaine's students, they feel frustrated when they don't win the prize.

This team represents the fourth category of procrastinators, the *Rebel*. Unless a task makes sense to rebels, they will not follow others' instructions. If the task is assigned by a teacher or parent, it will likely be put off as long as possible. Only when rebels come face-to-face with the negative consequences of their resistance will they begin the task.

Tyler

Tyler has always been strong willed. His parents joke that his first spoken word was no. Anything they asked of him had to pass the "makes sense to Tyler" test or he considered it a waste of time and postponable.

Tyler has plenty of energy and willingness for his own projects. Once he turned sixteen, he took over all car-related duties for the family: washing, waxing, detailing inside and out. He even learned how to change the oil and other fluids. It made sense to him that if he was going to drive the car, it should look and perform great. Other duties, like mowing the lawn, seem absolutely pointless to Tyler, and he drives his parents crazy by resisting doing them for as long as he can. The only way his father could get him to mow the lawn, for example, was to ratchet up the consequence of not mowing it—withholding the car keys on Tyler's prom night.

To Tyler, people who give in too easily are like sheep, without independence or identity. Tyler could allow himself to give in to what he felt was an unfair or stupid task only if he was faced with a price that was too high.

What the rebel values is independence—thinking for yourself, being in control of your own life as opposed to letting others control you. The rebel is an independent free thinker and won't do things like follow rules just because they are there. For you to follow a rule, it must seem fair and sensible to you.

In school, you'll procrastinate on any assignment that seems constricting or petty, even if it's worth a big portion of your grade. You'll put off studying until the morning of the test. On the other hand, if the assignment is engaging and reasonable, you'll do it right away. To you, this may demonstrate that your procrastination problem is your "stupid" teacher's fault.

For the rebel, ownership of the task is very important. If the idea to clean your room is yours, you approach it with enthusiasm. But if a parent comes by and says something like "Glad to see you're taking initiative," you may feel like your idea was just stolen. You may put off the task, thinking, *I'm not going to give them the satisfaction of doing what they say.* You might want to start an exercise program, for example, or improve your eating habits, but if others are telling you that you should do those things, you put off starting anything.

If you get that summer job waiting tables at the pizza shop despite your procrastination filling out the application, you may run into problems with the manager, who keeps giving you little tasks that are really the bussers' job. *I'll clean that section later,* you think, *after I've taken care of my customers.* In every situation where someone else is deciding what you should do, you just can't perform enthusiastically. It's against your principles. Even going along with your friends' ideas of what to do or where to go can feel like surrendering to an enemy.

To the rebel, independence is the most important thing a person can have. Cooperating with others when their requests are unfair, unreasonable, or uninteresting feels like giving away your soul. Any task that makes you feel obligated— rather than inspired—will be postponed.

A rebel's core value is independence

Are you a rebel? Read the following ten statements. If half or more of them ring true, you're a rebel and it significantly contributes to procrastination.

If I don't think something is fair, I won't do it.

I don't think people appreciate what I do get done.

People think I'm stubborn.

The more pressure people put on me to do something, the less likely I am to do it.

If someone wants me to do something that seems silly to me, I won't do it.

If I'm committed to something, I'll get it done no matter what.

I often think people are bossy and controlling.

I'll disagree with people just for the sake of disagreeing.

I'm easily annoyed when something or someone gets in the way of what I want to do.

I'm an independent thinker.

You can also take the *Am I a Rebel?* quiz at http://www .newharbinger.com/35876.

The rebel's passion for independence can fuel a life of accomplishment and unique character. Yet if the path to get there cannot be traversed alone and requires following instructions or cooperating with others, the rebel can get stuck. If you are so attached to self-direction that you cannot benefit from the direction of others, you can miss out on the very independence you desire.

• • • • • • • • •

These are the four types of procrastinators, each with their own style of procrastination, each with a unique way of thinking and feeling. Are you the perfectionist, who has to get things right; the warrior, who must feel fully engaged; the pleaser, who must keep everyone happy; or the rebel, who resists cooperation with others?

Don't be too quick to answer. There's some of each procrastination type in all of us. I'm a perfectionist/pleaser and my husband is a warrior/rebel. Whether you are one pure type or a hybrid, you will benefit from understanding them all. To further that understanding, in the next chapter we'll reveal the unique way each of these types think.

Chapter 6

Root Beliefs

Procrastination, like other problem behaviors, often results in regret. Faced with a missed deadline or lost opportunity, how many of us have complained, *What was I thinking*?

Chances are when you procrastinate you are thinking something along the lines of *I'll do it later; there's plenty of time;* or *I can't do it now because...* These are typical *task-avoidant thoughts,* thoughts that rationalize why the task can wait. Task-avoidant thoughts not only justify postponing the immediate task, but used often enough, they also keep you from achieving your larger goals. You won't pass your driver's test, get a summer job, or get into college thinking, *I'll do it later.*

Task-avoidant thoughts are unreliable guides for our behavior; however, they form in our heads so quickly and automatically, and in such variety, that it is very difficult to challenge them one at a time. In working with clients, I find it most effective to dig a little deeper at the roots of the tree, where we'll find the beliefs, often hidden, that feed our task-avoidant thoughts. These *root beliefs* are at the heart of the procrastination problem.

Let's revisit our four procrastinators and examine the root beliefs that are unique to each type, and the task-avoidant thoughts that spring from them.

The Perfectionist

Jordan was in a panic over his English term paper, a critical essay of *The Sound and the Fury*, which, according to him, was "the most challenging book I ever read." The questions he had to address about the author's use of stream of consciousness, or the themes of lost reputation and religious faith, weren't the kinds of things Jordan, who excelled in subjects like algebra and Spanish, normally thought about. Althought it wasn't his strongest area, Jordan was certainly smart enough to write the essay. I asked him what would happen if he just wrote what he was thinking.

"I could get it wrong," Jordan answered. "I don't know what the teacher wants to hear."

Me: What would happen if your teacher thinks you're wrong?

Jordan: She'll give me a bad grade.

Me: And then what would happen?

Jordan: I could get a C in English. Do you have any idea what that would do to my GPA?

Me: And if your GPA went down?

Jordan: I won't get into a good college. Everyone will know I've failed.

Jordan's root belief was now in plain sight. He thought that if he made a mistake he'd be a failure and lose the respect of others. To secure his standing in his tribe, Jordan operated under the principle *I must not make mistakes.*

This is the underlying belief of all perfectionists. It colors all your thoughts, raising the stakes for even the simplest of tasks. In the branches of the thought tree illustration on page 37 are some of the task-avoidant thoughts that are triggered whenever you are faced with a task that you aren't sure can be done perfectly. As the illustration shows, a tree with roots and branches like this is bare. When the only work you can display is what turns out perfect, there won't be much to show.

To the perfectionist, making a mistake equals failure.

But might not these task-avoidant thoughts be accurate? Could Jordan's root belief be true in this situation?

Possibly. Jordan could write an essay that his teacher would grade low enough to drag down his entire GPA— downgrade it so much that he couldn't get into a decent college. Jordan couldn't be sure. What Jordan could be sure about was that the longer he continued to act on his root belief and its task-avoidant thoughts, the less time he'd have to complete, and hopefully excel at, the essay.

Exercise: Identifying Your Task-Avoidant Thoughts and Root Beliefs

1. Think of something you have been putting off and write it down. This may be a chore, an assignment, talking to someone about something, physical exercise, or another type of self-care.

2. Now ask yourself: *Why don't I get started right now? If I did start, what am I afraid of? What's the worst thing that could happen if I started right now?* List the first answers that pop into your mind. These answers will most likely be your task-avoidant thoughts.

3. Once you have a few thoughts listed, circle one of them that feels especially true or upsetting, or both. (Jordan's most upsetting thought was that he might get a bad grade.)

4. Ask yourself, *If this thought came true, what is the worst thing this could mean about me? About my life? About my future?* Write down the answers.

5. Repeat step 4 until you have identified the belief at the root of your thought tree.

To help you do this exercise, download the *Root Beliefs* worksheet at http://www.newharbinger.com/35876.

The Warrior

On Thursday after school Emily decided to clean her room. Her friends were coming over for a sleepover on Friday, and she wanted to have a comfortable space for them. But then there was a post about a YouTube video on rock climbing and that, of course, couldn't wait. After the video, she noticed she was hungry and thought, *I'll have more energy if I eat first.* Then she got a call from a girlfriend about a sale at the mall. *Plenty of time to clean my room*, Emily thought. When she got home from the mall, her mother chastised her for missing dinner with the family again. Emily felt agitated. Cleaning her room didn't sound so appealing, and when she got a text inviting her to play with friends online, she thought, *I'll chill with a game for a while first.* A couple of hours later, Emily realized it was bedtime. *Well, I'm too tired now. I'll clean up tomorrow right after school.* In the end, Emily shoved everything under her bed and into her closet minutes before her friends arrived.

As long as stimulating activities were available, Emily didn't feel motivation for tasks that didn't engage her fully. Yet she genuinely wanted to have a clean room for her friends. What was the root belief stopping her from focusing on what she needed to get done? To find out, I asked Emily what would happen if she cleaned her room first, rather than watching the video.

Emily: I know that when I don't feel like doing something, I don't do it well. I really wanted to see the video and post it to my rock-climbing friends. I'd feel like I was missing out on that.

Me: And what if you had continued with cleaning your room despite these concerns?

Emily: I would have felt bored and irritated and that I was missing out.

Me: And if you had kept cleaning the room anyway?

Emily: I just couldn't. Watching the video felt more important, and it wouldn't take long. Cleaning the room would have taken hours, and it didn't have to be done until the next day.

Emily's root belief was starting to reveal itself. Emily thought that feeling a sense of excitement about an activity meant it was more urgent. To warriors like Emily, tasks and activities that are stimulating and engaging take priority over those that aren't. Emily thought, at least unconsciously, that if a task didn't motivate her, it wasn't as important as whatever did. Like all warriors, Emily's root belief regarding tasks was *I must feel motivated.*

> The warrior believes that feeling motivated is necessary before taking action.

The belief that feeling motivated toward a task or an activity makes it a priority distorts all the warrior's thinking, giving rise to justifications for putting off anything that isn't fully engaging. Here is an illustration of the warrior's thought tree.

Those other activities felt so important to Emily that she postponed cleaning her room. Might they *be* more important? Posting about the YouTube video immediately might have given her more status with her rock-climbing friends. She enjoyed her snack, saved money at the mall, and totally dominated at her video game. Perhaps those were special experiences that couldn't be had again. Emily couldn't be sure whether having a clean room for her friends would have been worth missing those experiences or not. All Emily could be certain about was that as long as she believed *I must feel motivated,* she would continue to engage in whatever activities fully engaged her, postponing tasks that did not—even tasks important for her personal happiness.

The Pleaser

Athena came in to session one week with a downcast look and a slumping posture. Three weeks earlier, she had told her boyfriend she'd go camping with him and some of their friends. But she hadn't asked her parents for permission yet, and the trip was the next day.

Athena would not have put herself in a situation like this unless one of her core values were threatened. To help her discover what that core value was, I invited Athena to join me in a question and answer exercise. Note how each question I ask brings Athena a little deeper into her fear. This exercise the *downward arrow.*

Me: What would happen if you talked with your parents?

Athena: They'll be upset with me going on an overnight with my boyfriend, even in a group.

Me: And if they get upset, what would that mean to you?

Athena: They'll say no. And that I should have approached them right away, before it's all planned and everything.

Me: And if that were true, what are you afraid will happen?

Athena: I'll have made them angry and my boyfriend angry that I can't go.

Me: And if this is true, what will it mean to you?

Athena: Everyone will hate me! I'll feel alone!

Clearly, Athena's core value was threatened. She believed that to maintain her connection with her parents and her boyfriend she needed to keep them happy. Athena's root belief was *If I displease others I love, I will be rejected.*

The unconscious belief *I must not displease others* acts as a wellspring for the thoughts that come to mind automatically whenever you are faced with the possibility of disappointing anybody. On the following page is an illustration of the pleaser's thought tree.

**The pleaser thinks,
*If I displease others,
I will be rejected.***

As a pleaser, you can never be completely certain that displeasing others won't result in them rejecting you. What Athena *could* be sure of was that the longer she acted on her underlying belief *I must not displease others*, the more potential strain she was putting on her connection with her parents and her boyfriend.

The Rebel

Tyler came into a session very upset. He'd just been graded a 70 on his history term paper even though, in his words, it was genius work. I didn't doubt him. Tyler was undeniably clever.

Tyler's issue was the teacher's requirements for notating references and providing a bibliography. Documenting his research seemed unnecessary to Tyler, something that would just slow him down, so he kept putting it off. When the due date arrived, it was too late to reconstruct everything and he had to turn in the paper incomplete. "Why do teachers have to put such ridiculous restrictions on us?" Tyler asked. "All it does is make it impossible to write anything good!"

This example of underperformance was typical for Tyler, who belonged near the top of his class but was in danger of failing several subjects. Tyler's resistance to following instructions was keeping him from getting credit for his creativity and intelligence. To find out what was causing that resistance, I asked him what would have happened if he had tracked his references at the start.

> *Tyler:* I would have felt stupid. Doing busywork just because someone wants you to is demeaning.
>
> *Me:* What if you went ahead and did it anyway, even though it was demeaning?
>
> *Tyler:* I couldn't respect myself. I'm not a slave to be ordered around.

To Tyler, cooperating with an assignment that didn't make sense to him was equivalent to enslavement. With his personal independence at stake, it's easy to see why he resisted the task. Like rebels everywhere, Tyler believed that if he followed orders from others he would be subservient to them. If he wasn't in control of the task, he would be taken advantage of and diminished somehow. Tyler believed, *I must not give in to others.*

Believing that allowing someone to lead you threatens your independence will make all assigned tasks look daunting. Here is the thought tree of the rebel.

Would Tyler have lost some self-respect and integrity by doing his history teacher's "busywork"? In his own mind, yes, but how long that would last is unknown. What we do know is that if Tyler keeps believing that he must be in control of a task in order do it, his grades will continue to suffer, making his path to independence all the more difficult.

• • • • • • • • •

Procrastination is not a sign of weakness, poor character, laziness, or failure. Procrastination is a normal human reaction to tasks that challenge our core values. When the perfectionist is faced with a task where he could fail, the perfectionist's core value—excellence—is threatened. When the warrior tries to do something without feeling motivated, his core value—full engagement—is threatened. When the pleaser wants to say or do something that might displease or disappoint others, her core value—connection with them—is threatened. When the rebel is given a job that makes her feel controlled, her core value of independence is threatened.

When your core value is threatened, your root beliefs are activated. These beliefs are what feed the task-avoidant thoughts that rationalize your behavior.

Acting in accordance with task-avoidant thoughts and their root beliefs may seem to protect our core values, but it can make matters worse. What makes these thoughts so powerful? Why do we keep thinking we should avoid tasks that we know we'll eventually have to face? In the next chapter, I'll answer these questions by revealing the powerful dynamic that keeps us returning to the same short-term solution.

Chapter 7

The Procrastination Cycle

I must not make a mistake. I must feel motivated. I must not displease others. I must not give in to others. These root beliefs, examined in the light of day, don't appear so reliable. One might ask: *If our root beliefs aren't necessarily true, and they point us away from our goals and values, why do we believe them?*

Root beliefs have something going for them that ordinary thoughts don't have. They *feel* true. If it feels to you like a task might impede your quest for excellence, be unengaging and tedious, threaten your socials connections, or compromise your independence, you are going to want to put that task off.

What we're feeling when we think about a task is emotion. Emotions help us know whether it is safe or beneficial for us to proceed. Positive emotions about a task tell us *All's clear, full steam ahead!* Negative emotions are a signal that something is wrong. They act as enforcers of our task-avoidant thoughts.

If there is the risk of failure at a task, the perfectionist feels fear, anxiety, or perhaps confusion. These emotions enforce the task-avoidant thought *I'll do it when I'm clearheaded.*

If a task isn't engaging, the warrior feels bored, irritated, and restless. These emotions enforce the task-avoidant thought *It's not that crucial that I get it done now.*

If doing a task may displease a loved one, the pleaser feels apprehension, guilt, and shame. These feelings enforce the task-avoidant thought *I'll take care of them first; my needs can wait.*

If a task is assigned condescendingly or seemingly makes no sense, the rebel feels helpless, confused, and angry. These emotions enforce the task-avoidant thought *This is stupid; I'll do it later.*

> Procrastination delivers immediate relief from negative emotion, which acts as a reward for the behavior.

In the short term, procrastination delivers what you want most—immediate relief from a negative emotion. This quick relief acts as a reward for our behavior. When we are rewarded for putting off a task, we are more likely to put it off again the next time it appears.

Procrastination can be explained as follows:

1. You think about the task, which

2. triggers root beliefs and accompanying negative emotion, which

3. triggers task-avoidant thoughts, which

4. causes you to put off the task, *for which you are rewarded with relief.*

And when we factor in that other powerful agent of procrastination, distraction, we get into even more trouble. Distracting activities, like watching a movie or using social media, not only ease the negative emotions associated with the task but also elicit positive emotions, which makes putting off the task doubly rewarding.

Avoidance and distraction are the two complementary components of procrastination. When we are simultaneously pushed away from essential tasks by our negative emotions and pulled toward pleasant activities that make us feel good, we have a pretty lethal combination. I call it the *procrastination cycle.*

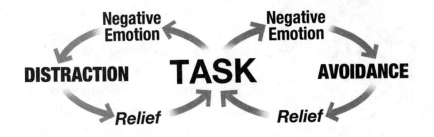

Neutralizing negative emotions and cultivating positive emotions isn't wrong or weak or stupid. For thousands of years, emotions have served us as reliable survival guides. The wild animal's howl or roar frightened our ancestors, warning them to stay alert. The chirping of crickets told them it was safe to relax. Neutralizing negative emotions and fostering positive ones is business as usual for human beings, and you are no exception.

The system fails when you're faced with a task that triggers negative emotions but is also crucial to your well-being. Putting off an essential task triggers *secondary negative emotions* that are just as difficult to neutralize as the ones you're temporarily relieved of. With procrastination, everything, including pain relief, is temporary.

For example, studying for an algebra exam can threaten the perfectionist with the possibility of errors, bore the

warrior, or, because it doesn't seem relevant, irritate the rebel. But if you avoid or distract yourself from studying, secondary emotions emerge. No amount of distraction can make you completely forget the upcoming test, and you are haunted by guilt and dread. Your postponed pain culminates on the night before the exam when, in addition to those two feelings, fear and panic set in. No amount of avoidance and distraction will work at this point. The only way to neutralize these emotions is to perform last-minute heroics, like pulling an all-nighter before the exam.

Although you can push a task to completion by harnessing your fear and panic as the deadline approaches, and you may pass the test, you have merely interrupted, not disrupted, the procrastination cycle. The next time the task of studying algebra arrives, you'll experience the same negative emotions and tendency toward distraction. Your underlying beliefs will still be intact. *I must not make a mistake, I must be stimulated, I must be in control.* The cycle is primed and ready for more repetitions.

Repeated failure to complete essential tasks on time and up to your ability will trigger deeper secondary negative emotions: frustration, regret, inferiority, anger with yourself, and worst of all, shame and depression. These are the most damaging and the longest-lasting consequences of procrastination. Sadly, when you're feeling ashamed and depressed, you cannot enjoy whatever excellence, social connection, stimulation, and independence you may have acquired already. And as long as you act on your underlying beliefs, you will be frustrated in your goal.

The most damaging and the longest-lasting consequences of procrastination are shame and depression.

Now that we've examined the core values, root beliefs, negative emotions, and behaviors that drive the procrastination cycle, we are ready to address what can be done about it. Each of the following chapters outlines a powerful tool that will help you master not only your procrastination but also your life. These tools will help you challenge your root beliefs, cope with negative emotions, and organize your difficult tasks to make them more manageable.

Of course, tools are only powerful in the hands that use them, and you'll need to be motivated to use them. One of the ironies of a self-help book about procrastination is that anything the author asks the reader to do is by definition a task, and breaking the cycle of procrastination is a big one. You have a lot of momentum going around and around the cycle, and it will require real thought and energy to change. You may be thinking, *There are enough things in my life waiting to be done. Don't give me any more!*

Because of this, I fully expect that some of you will decide you've done enough about the problem by reading this far, and that for now, your procrastination problem is manageable. You might even be thinking, *I'll work on my procrastination problem later.*

That's okay, because I firmly believe that while everyone has the potential to beat procrastination, you cannot do so unless you decide for yourself that the problem is one you're determined to tackle. That's why the next chapter is about recognizing when and whether completing a task will support your core value(s). Uncovering this personal incentive is the crucial first step to disrupting the cycle, and it will inspire you to do what you need to get done.

Chapter 8

Owning the Task

In my first session with Athena, she said her biggest problem
was completing her college applications. It was early
December of her senior year, and she was running out of time.
Her parents had worked together with her the previous spring,
helping Athena narrow her list to five schools, and most of her
friends had sent their applications in already. Her boyfriend
had the same first choice as she did, and he was impatient for

Athena to get hers in the mail. "I know I should apply, but I can't make myself do it," Athena told me. "I'm so ashamed!"

Many of us have been taught that by shaming ourselves and willing ourselves into correct behavior, we can master our to-do lists and broader obligations. If you rely on getting things done this way, you know that any success you enjoy will be short-lived. There is always another task waiting for your attention, requiring more shaming and willpower to push you through. Even if Athena were able to whip herself into applying for college, was she prepared to keep whipping herself forward for the next four years? Athena needed to have a solid motivation to move forward, and I wondered what that motivation could be.

"Why do you want to apply for college?" I asked.

Athena stared at me blankly. There was a long pause. "To make everyone happy," she said, and started to cry.

When Athena recovered enough to continue, the mystery of her procrastination unraveled. Athena had made some new friends at her summer job. Many of them were working and traveling instead of heading straight to college, an idea that excited her. Athena had no firm career plan yet, and she couldn't picture herself taking college classes that she wasn't sure she was interested in. Nor could she imagine continuing her commitment to her boyfriend after high school. A gap year seemed like a perfect way to meet new people and get new ideas about what she wanted to do with her life.

If you are shaming and pushing yourself to get things done, any success you enjoy will be short-lived.

Athena's procrastination problem wasn't with applying for college. What she was putting off was telling her parents and her boyfriend that she wasn't ready for it. Like all pleasers, she didn't want to disappoint anyone, and if she took ownership of the true task at hand—announcing her desire for a gap year—she was bound to disappoint.

As children, we are dependent on our parents for everything—food, shelter, and emotional support. We unconsciously adopt their values, trusting their guidance about what is good for us. As we grow, our dependency shifts to teachers and peers, until, as young adults, we take more control and responsibility for our own lives. As a teen, you're developing your own sense of what is important to you. You're harnessing your own unique motivations, preparing to take ownership of your life.

I asked Athena whether she wanted to take a closer look at her real procrastination problem: telling her parents and her boyfriend that she wanted to take a gap year after graduation. She said she did.

I suggested that Athena do a simple exercise designed to illuminate what advantages or disadvantages there were to putting off telling everyone her plans. It's called the *Procrastination Pros and Cons List*. I pulled up the whiteboard and drew a line down the middle. "Let's start with the pros," I said, handing her the marker. "What are the benefits to *not* telling everyone your gap-year plan?" Athena took the marker and began to write.

Pros to Procrastinating
I don't have to feel the anxiety of telling them.
I don't have to feel their disappointment or anger at me.
I don't have to deal with what others might think about my plan.

Athena's reasons for putting off telling her parents and her boyfriend what she wanted to do all shared a common theme: feeling anxious about disappointing them. To a pleaser like Athena, this was no small matter. When social connection is your core value, any task that threatens your connections will be avoided for as long as possible. We'd discovered the heart of the conflict that had kept Athena paralyzed for months.

I wondered whether there were any advantages for Athena to tell everyone her plans, despite the probability they'd be upset with her. To find out, I asked her to list the disadvantages of putting off the task. Here's what she wrote:

Cons to Procrastinating
Unless I tell them what I want to do, they'll keep bugging me about filling out the applications.
The longer I wait to tell them, the more upset with me they'll be when they find out.
I'm not standing up for what I want.
I'm not being honest with them.

On this side of the whiteboard, one example stood out. Athena valued honest relationships. Without honesty, her connection with her parents and her boyfriend wouldn't be worth much. This is the kind of motivation the pleaser needs to tap into to challenge procrastination. "When I think about not telling them as lying to them," Athena said, "I know I have to tell them."

Athena's procrastination pros and cons list revealed not only her problem but also its solution. When you can see clearly what is at stake, both for and against, your reasons to embrace a difficult task also become clearer. Athena was ready to take responsibility for what she needed to do, not for anyone else, but for herself. She was ready to own the task.

Before you attempt to use any tool in this book, be aware that unless the cons of procrastinating outweigh the pros, you are not likely to have sufficient motivation to move forward with it. And without a strong personal incentive to own the task, any efforts will likely fall short. Finding yours is the first step.

● ● ● ● ● ● ● ● ●

Let's look at how the issue of task ownership played out for Tyler, the rebel. Tyler hadn't done well on a history test because he had put off studying for it. But then his teacher offered him an opportunity to get extra credit to offset his poor grade, by writing an essay on the American president he most admired. This assignment did not inspire Tyler. Doing it, he said, would feel like jumping through hoops for the teacher.

Without a strong personal motivation to own the task, any efforts will likely fall short.

It sounded like Tyler was experiencing the normal rebel response to an uninspiring school assignment. I guessed that Tyler might benefit from looking at the pros and cons.

"Help me understand this," I said. "Will you write down all the good reasons you have for *not* doing the essay?"

Tyler liked this idea. It didn't take him long to list three great reasons to disown the task. When I asked him to list the cons to procrastinating, he had to think a little harder. But he came up with three good reasons why he shouldn't delay. When he finished, looking at the pros and cons side by side, Tyler had a new insight.

TASK	Writing extra-credit essay	
Pros to Procrastinating		Cons to Procrastinating
I don't have to do something I don't want to do.		I may end up with a bad grade in history.
I'll have more time to do things that I think are important.		Getting a lower GPA could decrease my chances to get into college.
I won't give the teacher the impression that I would jump through hoops for him to get a better grade.		I may regret not doing something that is not that hard to do.

One factor outweighed all the others. Writing the essay, even a mediocre one, would help his GPA and help his chances of getting into college. Tyler wanted to get out of his parents' house, hopefully even out of the state.

Tyler recognized that refusing to do the extra credit would hurt his progress toward his own goal. Now the assignment looked less like busywork and more like part of Tyler's master plan. He was ready to own the task.

Exercise: Procrastination Pros and Cons List

Is there a task you aren't sure you want to own? A helpful tool to help you decide is a *Procrastination Pros and Cons List*.

1. Think of a task that you have been putting off.

2. List all the advantages of procrastinating, for example, not having to do what is difficult or boring, not having to face possible failure, or not having to give in to others.

3. Next, list all the disadvantages of putting the task off, for example, feeling guilty, not being able to fully enjoy what you are doing while putting it off, not having time to do a good job on it, having to listen to people nag you about not doing it.

Once you have all the pros and cons listed, you can decide whether this task is something you want to own or not.

You can download a *Procrastination Pros and Cons List* at http://www.newharbinger.com/35876.

Remember that a pros and cons list is not a math exercise. You don't simply add up the reasons on each side and compare to find the winner. What you are giving yourself a chance to do by defining the pros and cons is to reveal (1) why you are avoiding it; and (2) what, if anything, would motivate you to embrace it. Both these questions will almost always center on the core value(s) of your type(s). The pleaser's need for connection, the rebel's need for independence, the warrior's need for full engagement, and the perfectionist's need for excellence are always at play when we put off doing what we need to do.

The beautiful thing about the core values that are hanging you up is that recognizing and claiming them is the key to finding the motivation you need to stop procrastinating. When Tyler recognized that the independence he craved could be furthered by writing an essay, he was ready to do it. Writing the essay became, in a sense, an act of rebellion against the forces that were keeping Tyler at home, under the thumb of his parents and teachers. Tyler had unleashed the rebel's hidden power, the drive for independence. His fear of "jumping through hoops" was not going to stop him now.

Similarly, nothing empowers the pleaser like deepening social connection. When Athena reminded herself that being honest with others is necessary for her to have authentic relationships, she found the motivation she needed to make her gap year come true. It wouldn't be easy, and feelings would get hurt, but Athena would be following the path her own heart dictated, not that of her parents and her boyfriend. If she couldn't do that, her connection with them would be neither authentic nor deep.

> **Recognizing and claiming your core values is the key to finding your motivation.**

What about the other types? Can the warrior own a task, even when it bores you? Yes, if completion of the task will bring you closer to a new level of engagement that you are aiming for. The skydiver's motivation to check all the seams and cords, then carefully fold and pack her parachute, doesn't spring from any inherent passion for the task itself, but from the promise of the full engagement that correct execution of the task will make possible.

Can the perfectionist own a task you aren't sure you can do well? Yes, when you recognize that uncertainty and risk are necessary for excellent outcomes to happen. The value of any accomplishment is proportional to the risk involved, whether it is the risk of making mistakes, failing, or being embarrassed in front of others. When the pros and cons are laid out in front of you, the prospect of excellence will become more clear and the choice more evident.

I understand that as a modern teen you are assaulted with dozens of tasks coming from every direction every day. If you don't have the time for a pros and cons list, or the situation does not allow, take this shortcut. When you are presented

with a task you don't want to do, ask yourself whether your core value would be better realized if it were completed. It can be a quick source of motivation.

For example, every time Tyler is assigned a paper, given a chore, or simply asked to do something as a favor, he asks, *Will completion of this task bring me more independence than putting it off?* Regardless of who originally assigned the task, if the answer is yes, Tyler is ready to own the task.

Whatever your type, you can often find instant motivation for even the smallest task by asking yourself how it aligns with your core value. The perfectionist can ask, *Which will bring me greater potential for excellence: attempting this task or putting it off?* The warrior can ask, *Will this boring task open up possibilities for more engaging opportunities, or fewer?* The pleaser can ask, *Will doing this, or not doing this, lead me to a deeper connection with others?*

Task ownership, as I've described it here, is a mental exercise for reimagining a task, moving it from the category of "something I *should* get done" to "something I *want* to get done." This distinction highlights the crucial incentive you need to move ahead. Without it, any effort you make will be powered only by a sense of obligation and duty, hardly the sort of fuel you want to rely on for the challenging tasks that life holds for you. When you harness your core values—excellence, full engagement, connection, or independence—you'll be ready to get things done!

Owning the task is the first crucial step to disrupting the cycle of procrastination. The second step, however, is just as important. In the next chapter, I'll show you how to counteract the task-avoidant thoughts and root beliefs that may threaten to undermine you every step of the way.

Chapter 9

Letting New Beliefs Take Root

As you may recall, in chapter 6, Jordan was struggling with his English essay on *The Sound and Fury*. During one of our sessions, we did the *Procrastination Pros and Cons* exercise together. Jordan decided that putting the essay off would not serve him in any significant way, whereas starting on it right away would allow him more time to do it well, helping him get a better grade and perhaps even improve his GPA. Having a GPA that would help him get into a great college was what Jordan was all about; after all, his core value was excellence. "I totally want to own this essay," he told me. "That's the easy part. But when I think about doing it, I feel unconvinced that I can do it without screwing it up."

The Perfectionist

Like all perfectionist procrastinators, Jordan had a root belief that was hanging him up. It triggered both feelings that the task was a threat and task-avoidant thoughts that gave him reasons for putting the task off. Jordan's belief—*I must not make a mistake*—meant that he'd have to write a perfect essay, without mistakes, that was better than the others in his class. Because that wasn't likely, writing the essay challenged Jordan's core value of excellence. Holding on to this root belief, Jordan was bound to put the essay off no matter how much he wanted to own it.

In chapter 6 we visualized root beliefs supporting branches of task-avoidant thoughts. What if Jordan could visualize a different tree for himself? I got out the whiteboard and near the bottom, I wrote, *I am willing to make mistakes.*

"What if you believed this?" I asked.

Jordan shook his head. "I've spent my entire life avoiding them," he said. "If my core value is excellence, why would I want to make mistakes?"

Is it true that those who achieve excellence don't make mistakes? Are perfectionists always perfect? Watching a ballerina perform, you might be tempted to think so. But had you attended any of her rehearsals, you would have witnessed the countless missteps and stumbles, lurches that should have been leaps, and yes, even the hard falls she endured to gain any outward appearance of perfection.

The same holds true for other figures of excellence—artists, musicians, inventors, scientists, and entrepreneurs. Not only do high achievers make mistakes, but also there is considerable evidence that they are *more* willing to make mistakes than underachievers. This is because doing things wrong is a great way—sometimes the only way—to learn how to do things right.

As successful people in all walks of life have shown us, to achieve anything worthwhile we must be willing to take risks. When you don't acknowledge failure as an option, you can only allow yourself to do tasks that you already know you can do well. How much more will you accomplish when you replace your *I must not make mistakes* belief with *I am willing to make mistakes*?

> Doing things wrong is sometimes the only way to learn how to do things right.

Jordan was intrigued. We spent the rest of the session sketching out a new thought tree, one with a willingness to make mistakes at the root. I've re-created it here, with refinements that make it universally useful for all perfectionist procrastinators.

The Warrior

Let's examine the root belief of the warrior: *I must feel motivated*. While it's true that the warrior thrives on excitement and competition, and performs best in situations that require full engagement of body and mind, is there any path in life that has a constant supply of such situations?

Emily loved rock climbing because it required all her strength and attention. When she was on a rock wall, she was in the zone, focused and strong without a care in the world. Yet preparing for a climb was a real challenge. Her friends would usually be outside honking the horn while she scrambled to collect her gear, and when they arrived she usually had to borrow some crucial piece of equipment she had forgotten to pack. Preparation for a climb wasn't fully engaging to Emily, so she put it off until there wasn't time to prepare properly. As a result, she had to borrow gear constantly, her performance suffered, and she wasn't being invited to more challenging outings with the advanced climbers.

The most exciting vocations in life require both regular preparation and reflection. A skydiver scrutinizes and packs his or her parachute carefully. The police officer may wait for hours to nab a suspect and then must write a report. The quarterback studies the playbook before the game and watches the film afterward. And as every soldier will tell you, it's 99 percent waiting for the 1 percent engagement.

To advance from one fully engaging situation—where your motivation is something you can feel—to the next is the warrior's greatest challenge. Can the warrior bridge the chasm of boredom?

Can the warrior bridge the chasm of boredom between one fully engaging activity and the next?

Just as a mountain climber makes a camp each night in the quest to conquer a challenging peak, the warrior must attend to the less exhilarating tasks that support the greater goal. What would happen if you decided that, when completion of the task will get you closer to your goal, you can act without feeling motivation? Can you focus on the mountaintop to make it up the hill? Are you willing to give up distractions to get where you want to go?

Here is a new thought tree for the warrior who is willing to act without necessarily *feeling* motivated. Imagine the things you can get done with a root belief like this.

The Pleaser

What if your root belief is *I must not displease others*? While it's true that disappointing your friends, family, or teachers could threaten your connection with them, ask yourself how deep a social connection is if, to maintain it, you cannot be authentic.

This was the price Athena was paying when, to accommodate others, she continually put off activities and tasks she genuinely wanted to do. When she went to the concert with her boyfriend instead of staying home to pack, read her camera manual, and get a good night's sleep, she was not only denying her own needs, but she was also hiding how much her new camera and her mountain retreat with her family meant to her. How could her boyfriend see Athena for who she is when she was pretending to be somebody else?

This authenticity problem followed Athena everywhere throughout her day. Expressing an unpopular opinion or making a decision that affected others were things to avoid. What if she was perceived as selfish or just plain wrong?

Whether she was helping a friend with homework instead of doing her own, skipping her guitar practice to drive her brother to his soccer practice, or going to parties to please her friends instead of relaxing by herself, Athena was not being honest, either with herself or with others. Sometimes she felt angry and alone even in the middle of a friendly crowd. As hard as she was working to stay connected, Athena wasn't getting the deep connection she craved.

If you're a pleaser, you'll recognize this irony in your own life. Despite

> Can you trust that your relationships will survive if you put others' needs on hold and take care of the tasks you need to do?

your best and most heroic efforts, inevitably you feel deprived of the intimacy you value most. What would happen if you believed that it is more important to find your own happiness than to keep everyone else happy? Can you trust that your relationships will survive if you put others' needs on hold and take care of the tasks you need to do?

Here is an illustration of a thought tree Athena and I designed to help her execute the tasks she decided to own. If you're a pleaser, you'll recognize the difference from the tree in chapter 6 right away. It all starts at the root belief *I am willing to displease others.*

The Rebel

Last, we have the rebel, whose underlying belief is *I must not give in to others.* When you accept an assigned task that you don't think is fair or necessary, are you surrendering your independence? Tyler believed he was. He believed it so strongly that he put off tasks he knew he'd need to do to get what he wanted. Going to college and getting out of his parents' house, for example, would require graduating with decent grades, something he couldn't do if he put off required classes he thought were unnecessary and postponed doing assignments he thought were stupid until it was too late to do a good job on them.

If completion of a task is necessary for you to meet your personal goals, and you put the task off for fear of surrendering to others, what you may be surrendering is your future independence. Tasks that are not to your liking are like hurdles for a runner. You need to jump over them to win the race!

Does this mean the rebel must say yes to every task, order, request, or ultimatum? Certainly not. But if your default answer is no to whatever is asked of you, try reviewing the pros and cons. What if completion of the task will serve your interests? Just because you're assigned a task, or don't agree with it, doesn't mean you won't benefit from getting it done.

> Just because you are assigned a task, or don't agree with it, does not mean you are giving up your independence.

Once Tyler decided to own the task of writing that extra-credit essay on the American president he most admired, he needed to adopt a new root belief about tasks. What if he replaced *giving in to others* with *cooperating with others*? Compromise and

75

cooperation are helpful skills for every goal, including personal independence and integrity. Ask the master chef who started out busing tables, or the Supreme Court justice who began as a law clerk. For Tyler, and for all rebels, a better rule to operate by is "If the task will serve my long-term interests, *I am willing to cooperate with others.*"

Here's a thought tree with the rebel's new and improved underlying belief at the root. How much progress toward your goals could you make if you adopted it?

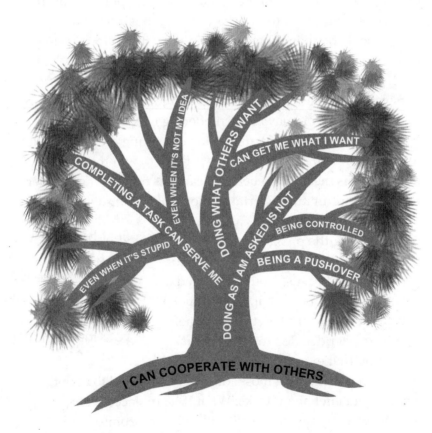

Remember that planting a new root belief will not automatically uproot the old one. Just as a tree must receive water and sunshine, your new belief must be nurtured at every opportunity. By nurturing I mean for you to practice holding the new belief in your mind when you are thinking about the problem task. Your old root belief will continue to express itself, but don't try to quiet it. Just allow it to play in the background like a song you've gotten tired of.

> Practice holding your new root belief in your mind, while allowing the old belief to play in the background like a song you've gotten tired of.

With practice, your new belief will take root, and the conflicts with the tasks you've been procrastinating on will become less threatening. When the perfectionist is willing to make mistakes, the warrior willing to engage without feeling motivated, the pleaser willing to disappoint others, and the rebel willing to cooperate when it will serve him or her, each will create new experiences that cannot happen within the procrastination cycle. This new experience will confirm and support your new, more expansive belief. You will find yourself both capable and willing to perform a much wider range of tasks, and in the process, you'll move closer to accomplishing your personal goals.

You can download a *Planting Root Beliefs* worksheet to practice with at http://www.newharbinger.com/35876.

This brings up a question: How can you act on a new root belief when you're experiencing emotions that make the old root belief feel true? We'll examine that in the next chapter.

Chapter 10

Riding the Wave

Tyler came into a session one day very upset. He'd been marked absent so many times for gym that if he missed it once more he was going to fail. Failing the course would mean he'd have to make it up during his senior year or he wouldn't be allowed to graduate. That was enough motivation to allow him to own the task of showing up for class, but it didn't stop him from hating it. All through the class he was thinking task-avoidant thoughts like *Why should I have to waste a whole period playing dodgeball or doing laps?* and getting angrier and angrier.

Tyler's outrage at being forced to attend a class he thought was unnecessary is a good example of how our task-avoidant thoughts come with some very compelling negative emotions attached. When a task is in direct conflict with one of our core values—in Tyler's case, it was his independence—we feel bad. The negative emotions vary depending on the core value that is threatened, but they include anxiety, boredom, irritation, confusion, and embarrassment, to name a few. These emotions can also be experienced as physical sensations, like tightness in your chest, an upset stomach, or a rapid heartbeat. While your underlying beliefs and task-avoidant thoughts trigger your procrastination, your negative emotions and feelings are what enforce it.

When we experience negative emotion, our natural reaction is to move away from whatever is causing it. There is a good reason for this. Negative emotions signal threat. Our fear of bears tells us not to approach and pet them. Avoiding activities and tasks that feel threatening has helped us survive for thousands of years. Negative emotions serve us very well until we begin to serve them.

Underlying beliefs trigger task-avoidant thoughts. Negative emotions enforce them.

Emotions can be relied upon as a guideline, but not as a boss. In a complex modern world, negative emotion is often an unreliable indicator that a task is a real threat. Tyler's anger at being pressured to go to gym wasn't a reliable signal that his independence was threatened. In fact, going to gym was a necessary step toward Tyler's future independence. In this case, Tyler's feelings were an obstacle rather than an aid.

When you decide to own a task that threatens your core value, although you may be cultivating a new root belief that you can handle the threat, you are still going to feel like something is wrong. That is the central dilemma for each of the four types of procrastinators.

The Perfectionist: I'm not sure I can do this correctly. If I try and I fail, I'll feel anxious, afraid, humiliated, and confused.

The Warrior: This is boring. If I keep doing it, I'll feel irritated, powerless, and restless.

The Pleaser: If I tell them what I really think, I'll feel apprehension, guilt, and shame.

The Rebel: This makes no sense. If I do it, I'm going to feel angry, helpless, and frustrated.

No matter how determined you are to own a task, when negative emotions flare up, you'll want to put off the task to make those emotions go away. That's the only way they'll go away, right?

Wrong. What we forget when stuck inside the procrastination cycle, avoiding and distracting ourselves from negative emotion, is that all emotions have a beginning, a middle, and an end. Your fear of making a mistake or displeasing somebody, your boredom with an unstimulating task, your rage at being told what to do, are all normal emotions that our bodies and our minds have whipped up for us. But they don't last forever. And you can handle them.

I grew up in Hawaii and going to the beach was a regular activity for our family. I remember as a little girl wading into the surf and seeing an approaching wave that was higher than my head. Instinctively, I stiffened up and braced myself, only to be slapped down by the wave. I scrambled to shore, coughing up water, much to the delight of my older sister.

All emotions have a beginning, a middle, and an end.

After she was done laughing at me, my sister showed me how to dive straight into a wave and let it wash over me. She showed me how to relax my body and float on top of the waves. Eventually, I discovered that I could swim right along with a wave and ride it in to the shore.

Emotions are like ocean waves. You can try to resist them and be slapped down again. Or you can learn how to ride them and get things done. How much more could you accomplish if, rather than avoiding unpleasant emotions, you rode them like a surfer does a wave?

To understand how to ride the wave of negative emotion, let's look at what you're probably doing now, which is much like what a novice does when wading into the ocean for the first time. When faced with uncomfortable feelings, it's natural to tense the body. We hunch or slump, and we breathe more shallowly, trying, in effect, to resist the feeling. While this may bring some short-term relief, the next wave is building momentum, and you are right in its path.

Emotions are relentlessly persistent. How often do we tell ourselves, *I'll do this later, when I feel like it*? But we never end up feeling like it. In fact, the more you suppress a feeling now by avoiding a task, the more like it will be to rear its ugly head the next time. When the uncompleted task comes back to haunt you, negative emotion rises again, strong as ever. Our resistance only postpones the pain.

If resistance is futile, then how do we "ride" a wave of emotion? Fortunately, you have a built-in tool for that: your breath.

Resist feelings and be slapped down again and again.

Breathing for Balance

The next time you begin a difficult task that you've decided to own, rather than tensing up and resisting whatever emotion you are feeling, try this simple technique. Open your mouth and breathe in. Draw the air deep into your lungs so that your belly expands. Straighten up and fill the tops of your lungs, too. Make lots of space for the emotion. Then, as you breathe out, imagine yourself giving up control of the feeling.

This technique, called *diaphragmatic breathing*, is how you ride a wave of emotion. Here's how it works: When faced with any kind of threat, not only physical threats but also threats to a core value, your nervous system goes into what is known as the *fight-or-flight reflex*. This reaction is characterized by negative emotions and physical changes like sweating, dry

83

mouth, a faster heartbeat, and faster, shallower breathing. It is unlikely that you notice these symptoms; they happen automatically. And because they are beyond our direct control, we tend to deal with them by avoiding what has triggered them. If it's a threatening task, we put it off.

If you've decided to own the task, however, you'll want to ride this wave, and your breath is how you stay balanced on your board. When you breathe deep into the belly, slowly and deliberately, you send a message to the brain that says, *I can handle this.* Breathing deeply and purposefully in response to a negative emotion, in effect, tells your body and brain to relax and allow the feeling to run its course. You will not be acting to stop it. You are cultivating one or more of your new root beliefs: *I can make mistakes, I can act without feeling motivation, I can disappoint others,* and *I can cooperate with others*!

As you breathe in, make lots of space for the emotion. As you breathe out, imagine yourself letting go of control.

While riding the wave, if you notice any part of your body that feels particularly uncomfortable, you can inhale directly into that area, making more space for the discomfort. Remember that you are not trying to get rid of anything; you are simply allowing whatever feeling that may arise to be there. The feeling may intensify, it may move to different parts of your body, it may change into another feeling, or it may decrease. Whatever it does, just continue to breathe and make space for whatever feelings happen. If you do, I promise that the feeling will change. Like the ocean waves, emotions ebb and flow.

Of course, emotions, like waves, come in all sizes. Some are big enough to knock you off balance. But if you want to get the things done that you need to get done to live the life you want, then you won't let that stop you.

Back in Hawaii, sometimes the power and speed of a wave caught me by surprise, and I was thrown under and tossed like a piece of seaweed in the churning water, and repeatedly slammed against the ocean floor. There was nothing to do but relax my body and surrender until it had passed. I came up gasping for air, speckled with sand burns, and a bikini bottom full of sand, but I was alive and I knew in my heart *it was worth it.*

When you breathe deeply, slowly, and deliberately,
you send a message to the brain that says, I can handle this.

Learning to ride your waves of emotion is worth it, too. You can practice anytime. To help you, you'll find an audio file with guided *Ride the Wave* instructions downloadable at http:// www.newharbinger.com/35876.

Riding the wave will build resilience to the number one thing that fuels the procrastination cycle: negative emotion. The next chapter deals with the number two fuel for the cycle. It's an especially difficult problem for modern teens.

Chapter 11

Eliminating Distractions

How many times have you gotten stuck for information while writing a paper, then whipped out your smartphone and googled it? The smartphone is the most versatile information resource in history, indispensable for today's student. Yet when it comes to task completion, the smartphone is your frenemy.

Unlike your parents when they were in high school, whenever you are working on a task, you must contend with phone calls, texts and tweets, email, Skype, and dozens of other social media alerts, all saying the same thing: *Look at this now! What you're doing can wait!* And when the task you're working on is an uncomfortable one for you—threatening your excellence, social connection, engagement, or autonomy— the temptation to pick up your smartphone can feel irresistible.

If Athena didn't answer the text from her boyfriend right away, he might think he wasn't important to her. If her girlfriend posted a selfie on Instagram, she needed to praise it immediately or risk hurting her feelings. Everyone in her wide circle of friends knew Athena would be sympathetic to their problems, so she had numerous requests for her attention throughout her day. With all those interruptions, Athena never seemed to have enough time to study for school, to relax with a book, to practice her guitar, or even to sleep at night. If you're a pleaser like Athena, whose connections to others is your most precious value, failing to respond to your social-media feed can make you very anxious.

Emily's habit of picking up her phone in the middle of a task was based on her need to be in the center of the action. How could she focus on a boring reading assignment when she knew the latest social media post might be about a friend's amazing rock-climbing accomplishment? And what exciting or important development might she be missing while she was doing her laundry? If Emily didn't check her phone every five minutes, she felt she might miss out on something exciting that would fully engage her. And if her social feeds didn't satisfy, movies and YouTube videos were only a few clicks away. If you're a warrior like Emily, your smartphone offers reliable escape from deadly boredom to lively engagement.

When Jordan was faced with a task he couldn't be sure he'd do well at, relief was as close as his smartphone. When texting his friends or monitoring Twitter feeds, the pressure to do things perfectly disappeared and he could relax. And because the Internet is the best place to do research, Jordan always had an excuse to go online. Once he'd googled something—the meaning or spelling of a word, for example—it was easy to hop around to other sites to get more ideas. This process could consume hours of his time, so that when he finally got around to working he was getting sleepy. If you're a perfectionist like Jordan, who thinks you need to be clearheaded to do good work, you may often put off homework until tomorrow, when you'll be fresh and rested.

When it comes to task completion, the smartphone is your frenemy.

When stuck with an assigned task he didn't like, Tyler was easily distracted by his phone. The moment he picked it up, the chore or the homework disappeared and Tyler was in a world of his own, unreachable to his parents and other figures of authority. Why be trapped feeling like an anonymous drone when he could get updates on his favorite sports team, watch a funny video, or discover a hot new band? If you're a rebel, you may feel the same.

Regardless of what type of procrastinator you are, when you have a task that threatens your core value, you don't feel safe and are even more vulnerable to distractions than usual. Whether the impulse to pick up the smartphone is based on a need to please, to feel engaged, to avoid making a mistake, or to feel independent, it is, for most teens, the single biggest obstacle to getting things done. So, short of turning your phone off, what can you do to make it less distracting?

Limit how often you check your email, text messages, and social media.

The first and most essential thing you can do anytime you are working on a task is to limit how often you check your email, text messages, and social media. The more often you stop to check, the less productive you're likely to be. When you do need to check, set a timer for yourself to remind you to get back on task. If you are unable to monitor yourself this way, consult the following list of stronger measures.

Before engaging in any challenging task, here are a few steps you can take to prevent smartphone distractions:

- Go to your settings and turn off all notifications, alerts, sounds, and vibrations—or simply switch to airplane mode.

- Send a group text to everyone who is important to you, saying, *I will be working on my social science paper for the next 90 minutes and will not be available.*

- Store your phone in a place beyond your immediate reach—in a drawer, perhaps, or better yet, in another room.

As an alternative to these measures, there are a host of new apps coming out to help us manage the distraction of smartphones. These apps block whatever media you select for as long a period as you choose. Some even enable you to schedule recurring distraction-free sessions in advance.

Although adjusting phone settings and getting antidistraction apps takes some extra effort up front, you will notice a world of difference working at tasks without the interruptions of social media. And the messages that accumulate during your work session will be more satisfying for you to respond to when you know you have gotten something done.

Other Distractions

Of course, smartphones are not the only distraction you face every day. Hunger and thirst are compelling reasons to stop whatever you're doing and make a trip to the kitchen, and once you're there, who knows what other distractions will appear? Emily often became so absorbed in whatever game she was playing or music she was dancing to that she skipped meals. Then when she got around to her reading assignment, which did not fully engage her, within a few minutes she was hobbled by low-blood-sugar fatigue. Her solution? Keep a supply of energy bars—the same fuel she used for rock climbing—in her desk drawer, so when the hunger urge hit she could stay on task without leaving her room.

If you're working at home, other family members can be distracting, especially for the pleaser. Athena's mother might call for her help with housework or unloading groceries any time of day, and her younger sister had a habit of showing up at Athena's door whenever she had a problem or something exciting to share. Athena felt that not responding would be perceived as rude and uncaring—which could jeopardize her connection to them—so when she was interrupted by her family she always set aside whatever task she was on. Between her friends and her family, Athena was like an emergency first responder, on call 24/7.

Athena's solution was to design a "Studying—Do Not Disturb. Thank You!" sign to post on her door whenever she needed to create some space for herself. When things got especially hectic at home, she grabbed her backpack and headed off to the library or her favorite coffee shop. It was scary for her to make herself unavailable and risk disappointing them, but Athena reminded herself that she deserved time to herself and that being authentic with her family was necessary for a true connection. As a bonus, Athena was surprised by how good she felt when she took care of herself.

If others are distracting you from a task, change your environment.

The list of things that can distract us is, of course, infinite. Anything that feels less painful than the task at hand can grab our attention—even other tasks. When Tyler was assigned to trim the hedges one Saturday, a half-hour job, he devoted an hour to organizing the toolshed instead. What made a chore like organizing the toolshed attractive enough to qualify as a distraction? Simple. It was Tyler's idea.

Emily so dreaded the boredom of picking up that she'd rather do twenty pushups than push a vacuum around her room. And when Jordan sat down to write a short creative essay, suddenly reviewing five chapters of social studies looked more appealing.

When you are faced with a task that threatens your core value, your perspective changes. Sights, sounds, smells, and thoughts beckon to you in new ways, promising relief from the uncomfortable feelings associated with the task. This phenomenon is bound to happen every time, so rather than allowing yourself to be blindsided, why not plan for it? The more you can anticipate distractions, the more practical steps you take to prevent them.

In the next chapter, I'll introduce a powerful tool to prevent a condition that all four types of procrastinators commonly face: being overwhelmed.

Chapter 12

Dividing Until Doable

A mason was pushing a wheelbarrow full of bricks down the road one day when he came to a rushing stream with a washed-out bridge. A man sitting by the side of the road laughed and said, "If you can get that load across, I'll eat my hat!"

After surveying the situation for a minute, the mason turned to the man and nodded. Without a word, he lifted a brick from the top of his load and, with a grunt, heaved it across the stream to the other bank. Picking up another brick, he repeated the process. A half hour later, he was fording the stream, dragging his empty wheelbarrow.

When the mason reached the other side, he restacked the bricks in the wheelbarrow. Before resuming his journey, he turned to the man on the other side, and shouted, "Eat it one bite at a time!"

Many tasks you're faced with will have the equivalent of a washed-out bridge, a seemingly impossible obstacle. When you are tempted to put off a task due to its size, complexity, or difficulty, I suggest you *divide it until doable.*

Begin by asking yourself, *How many parts can I break this task into*? The more, the better, because smaller tasks are more manageable. You're much more likely to complete a dozen "doables" than a single task that is perceived as *un*doable.

Jordan, our perfectionist, provides a good example of this. Faced with another essay in his English class, Jordan was feeling depressed. The subject this time was Shakespeare's *The Tragedy of Julius Caesar,* and the assignment was to write a persuasive argument in the voice of one of the characters. As usual with these kinds of projects, Jordan was sure he would screw it up and was having trouble getting started. Like all perfectionists, he thought he needed to know what he was going to say before he began.

The truth is, very few creative works start out fully formed in the creator's head. Jordan's essay would unfold gradually over many writing sessions. He needed only to address one aspect of the project during any single session. Working together, we divided Jordan's essay into "doables":

Day 1: *Pick a character.*

Day 2: *Research the character.*

Day 3: *Write an outline.*

Day 4: *Write one paragraph (repeat as necessary).*

With only one paragraph to write each day, Jordan could whittle away at the essay until it was done. Of course, this would be a whole new way of working for Jordan and would take some practice to get used to. Would he be able to treat his daily objectives as actual deadlines? Would he be able to risk making a mistake? Jordan would need to remind himself of his new root belief again and again. He'd be using his breath to ride numerous waves of negative emotion. These tools are needed every step of the way.

Emily was faced with a similar challenge cleaning her room. It looked like the aftermath of a hurricane, and Emily felt like she was going to lose precious hours of her day doing a task that bored and irritated her. She told me she didn't have that kind of stamina. She knew it wouldn't take much to distract her.

I told Emily I understood how she felt. If I had to climb one of the rock faces she climbed, it would seem impossible.

"That's because you're treating the whole climb as one thing," she answered. "I only think about it one foothold at a time. When I have a firm footing, I can rest and relax a bit before looking for the next one."

Emily was dividing granite bluffs into doable footholds to conquer them. Could she do the same for the less glorious task of cleaning her room? Here's the plan she came up with:

Doable 1: *Gather up all the dirty clothes and start a load of wash.*

Doable 2: *Collect all the dirty dishes and trash.*

Doable 3: *Vacuum and dust.*

Doable 4: *Fold and put away clothes.*

Doable 5: *Make bed, organize closets and drawers.*

Between each "foothold," Emily could relax a bit with something more engaging for her, like playing one level of a video game or chatting with friends. And as each part of the task was completed, the more manageable cleaning her room would appear.

When you take small action steps on something you are not feeling motivated to do, you'll almost always begin to feel more motivation once you've gotten started. Because you got something done, the next step does not seem as formidable. Just as each foothold brings the rock climber closer to attaining the peak and motivates her for the next foothold, each doable you master will help you "keep your eye on the prize" and embrace the next doable with a clear sense of purpose.

*You are more likely to complete a dozen
doable tasks than one undoable one.*

This may come as revelation to all procrastinators, and particularly warriors, who tend to act only when they feel motivated. The truth is, action *creates* motivation. Whatever the task, if you are feeling overwhelmed by it, when you divide it into doable tasks, you create not only more opportunities to act but also more opportunities to build motivation. Even simple tasks like doing the dishes can be more motivating when you break them down further. Try it the next chance you get. Wash the dish, not the dishes!

Exercise: Divide Until Doable

Think of a big task that you have been putting off, such as applying for college, getting a job, organizing your room, writing a term paper, or starting an exercise program. Instead of focusing on the end goal, think of at least five steps that will get you there. It is easier to approach something if it is broken down into parts.

For a downloadable *Divide Until Doable* form, go to http://www.newharbinger.com/35876.

Of course, just because doables are bite-size doesn't mean they will be easy to swallow. In the next chapter, I'll introduce a way you can pump up your energy for even the most forbidding task.

Chapter 13

Beating the Clock

Several years ago I decided to write a book on a subject I was passionate about: social anxiety for teens. I'd never written a book before, and when I researched how to get published I found out that to get a book contract I'd need to write a book proposal. But every time I sat down to write one, I felt overwhelmed. I changed it this way and that. I'd put it aside for a week and then come back to it. It took me a full year to write that proposal.

Happily, it caught the interest of a publisher and I got a book contract, complete with a series of deadlines for producing the manuscript. Every time I sat down to write, I felt all the familiar anxieties about getting it right, but thinking about the approaching deadline inspired me to let it flow. I ended up writing the entire book in the same amount of time it took to write the proposal!

As most of us have experienced, a ticking clock in the background can inspire us and help us focus. When your back is to the wall and you have nothing more to lose, you can sometimes do amazing things. It is evidence of the human spirit and when it happens, it certainly makes a great story. In fact, it's a central theme of the story of many procrastinators: *It's the only way I can get things done.*

Unfortunately, last-minute heroics have a downside. There is the long period of mounting worry and guilt that leads up to the deadline, time that could have been devoted to doing a better job than can be managed in the final hours when you are rushed, sleep deprived, and ill prepared. If only you could eliminate that painful escalation of the pressure. If only some of that last-minute inspiration that a deadline provides could be tapped into sooner, before the ax is about to fall.

It can. There is no reason you cannot create your own pressure-filled deadlines to help you focus on your doables. In fact, this is an essential tool for the procrastinator. I call it *Beat the Clock.* It's named after an old TV show where contestants were challenged to perform tasks while time was counted down on a large sixty-second clock. The show repeatedly demonstrated that any task can be made more motivating, as well as more entertaining, with an arbitrary time limit.

Beat the Clock has two simple components: a firm start time and a firm end time. These are decided on in advance so that while you're working on the task you don't have to think at all about how long to spend on it. All your attention can be focused on what you're doing, and what you're feeling while you're doing it. No matter how frustrating, irritating, or boring the task is to you, you know there'll be an end to it.

Create your own pressure-filled deadlines to help you focus.

Let's look at how Tyler's attitude about mowing the lawn changed when he turned it into a *Beat the Clock* challenge. Tyler hated to the mow the lawn, but his freedom was tied to the task. He would lose his car privileges if he did not do his chores. He estimated that the task could be done in as little as thirty minutes. So one Saturday morning after breakfast he pulled out the mower and set the timer on his phone for thirty minutes. Once the seconds started flashing away on the screen, Tyler felt himself rising to the challenge. He finished in twenty-eight minutes and twelve seconds. The next time the grass needed cutting, Tyler had a personal best to beat!

Here's why this worked: before Tyler attached his own personal goal to the task, mowing the lawn felt like a way for someone else—his father—to control him. It was his father's idea of what needed to be done, not his. Now, instead of

103

simply following his father's orders, Tyler was playing his own game. By allotting only thirty minutes to the task, he was mastering it rather than letting it master him. As a bonus, he was also clearing more free time for activities that were important to him.

Now let's look at what *Beat the Clock* can do for perfectionists. As you will recall, Jordan had a Shakespeare paper to write, which he had divided into doables. The first on the list was to choose a character for a point of view. Choosing anything presented challenges for Jordan, and this choice was no exception. *Which character would be best? Could it be a minor character or must it be a central one? A woman or a man?* There were so many variables. Jordan could go in circles indefinitely with a decision like this, putting off his decision until a day or two before the paper was due.

For perfectionists, who think they shouldn't start on anything unless they know they will do it correctly, or for anyone having difficulty get started, it's best to begin with a short work session. It helps take the emphasis off the outcome, tricking the mind into lowering its expectations. For Jordan, I suggested a special variation of the *Beat the Clock* tool that I call the *Five-Minute Jump-Start*. I set the timer on my watch for five minutes and asked him, "Okay, how about you choose that character right now?"

"Now?" Jordan asked, shifting in his chair uncomfortably. "I don't feel all that clearheaded today. I was up late last night."

I knew, of course, that Jordan was avoiding the task. He would never feel clearheaded enough for the job. We took a few minutes to review his root belief: *I am willing to make mistakes.* We reviewed how he would ride the wave of whatever feelings came up. I reminded him, "It's just five minutes."

Jordan sighed and shrugged. "I think I can manage that," he said.

After five minutes, the timer went off and Jordan looked up from his book.

> **The Five-Minute Jump-Start**
> 1. Set the timer for five minutes.
> 2. Do as much as you can in that time, not paying any attention to the quality of your work.
> 3. Pat yourself on the back for getting started!

"Okay, I've decided," he said, looking a little shaky. Naturally, he wasn't certain his choice was a good one. But now that he was acting as if he was willing to make mistakes, he felt okay about it. He was surprised how good it felt to get even this small thing done. For the perfectionist, *Beat the Clock* not only helps you get started, but it also keeps you from second-guessing everything you do.

The *Five-Minute Jump-Start* works great for starting all kinds of tasks—reading a book, planning a trip, even for the biggest most important challenges, like researching and choosing a college. The most fuel is burned getting a plane off the ground. Once you are airborne with a task, you'll have momentum, and your destination will feel more doable.

Warriors and rebels can also benefit from *Beat the Clock* time limits. Emily's room cleaning doable list was a perfect candidate for this tool. Rather than leaving her doables open-ended, she set a ten-minute limit for each one. If she didn't finish within ten minutes, she took a half-hour break before resuming the task, once again with a ten-minute time limit.

Because chores themselves weren't motivating for Emily, her motivation became the expectation of the free time awaiting her after the ten minutes of task time was up. With her doable completed, she could enjoy the things—gaming, chatting, or other distractions—guilt free, without being haunted by feelings of shame when she remembered her messy room. Emily was still bored and irritated with her room-cleaning doables, but never for more than ten minutes at a time. Like most of my clients who procrastinate, Emily could almost always ride the wave for ten minutes. And the more ten-minute sessions she racked up, the easier it became.

Sometimes when you play variations of *Beat the Clock*, you'll find yourself getting absorbed in the task. When you set a timer and create an external framework, you are less easily distracted, and more likely to become focused and motivated. If you find yourself wanting to work longer on a task than you planned, good! But I encourage you to continue to honor the time limit you've set, at least for a while. Stop and acknowledge what you've accomplished. This is not to assess the volume or quality of your work, but simply to acknowledge the fact that you applied yourself for the period of time you committed yourself to. This is a victory, an experience that will blaze new neurological pathways in your brain, pathways that support your new beliefs—*I am willing to make mistakes, I don't have to feel motivated, I don't need to be in control.*

Honor the time limit you've set. Stop and acknowledge what you've accomplished.

By sticking with your *Beat the Clock* time limit, you will also be preventing burnout. If you keep working until you are done, even if you feel motivated, you can become physically, mentally, and emotionally depleted. It can color your experience, making the next doable more imposing. It can also reaffirm the idea we must never stop working unless everything is done, which can turn any task into drudgery.

The more you play *Beat the Clock*, the more natural it will feel to use it as an antiprocrastination tool. If you have a smartphone that accepts voice commands, you'll find it's a snap to pull it out and say, "Set my timer for ten minutes."

Your smartphone won't only help you beat the clock, but it can help you beat the calendar, too. Read on and find out another great way to put today's technology to work for you!

Chapter 14

Staying on Schedule

At 1:15 p.m., your physics teacher announces there will be a test on the last two chapters during fifth period on Thursday next week. You make a mental note: *Gotta remember to study for that!* Now you are locked in, good to go, right?

Not exactly. By making that mental note, you created a new pattern of neurons in your brain; however, the electromagnetic pulses, or synapses, that connect those neurons fire randomly and quickly, as many as fifty times a second. The pattern that made up the mental note may exist in your brain for as little as one-fiftieth of a second before those neurons begin firing off about something more interesting, like meeting your friends for frozen yogurt after school.

For a memory to anchor itself, that pattern of neurons must be repeatedly reinforced. If you reminded yourself as you were leaving class, *Gotta remember, last two chapters fifth period on Thursday next week*, it would be a little more committed to memory than before. And if, while you were enjoying frozen yogurt with your friends, you all discussed the upcoming test, that would be even more helpful. If you made it your practice to systematically re-create neural patterns in your brain for every task that awaits you in the hours, days, weeks, and months ahead, you would indeed have everything locked down and good to go. You'd also be a very unusual person.

When you think about studying for that physics test next week, and you imagine the week ahead—seven twenty-four-hour days—it seems like a vast empty prairie with plenty of room to roam. Your natural thought is *I've got all the time in the world*.

Every modern teen, procrastinator or not, needs the help of an external guide, a reliable timeline where you can literally see that which you cannot picture in your head—where you stand in time. Although this guide can be in the form of a day planner or a wall or pocket calendar, in this chapter I'm going to focus on the turbocharged timeline you probably hold in your hand dozens of times a day: the calendar app on your smartphone. When you cannot keep mental track of all the your tasks and deadlines—and who can possibly do that?—the calendar app is indispensable.

Because we cannot possibly imagine an entire week of activity in our heads all at once, without an external visual timeline we cannot accurately judge how much time is available to us for any given task. To avoid the all-the-time-in-the-world illusion, enter *all* your commitments—not just the difficult tasks—into your calendar. With your classes, extracurricular activities, social plans, trips, and even personal downtime blocked out on your calendar in advance, whenever a difficult task appears, you can see at a glance which time blocks are still available to you. Then when you open your calendar app to schedule that study session for your physics test, you'll see a different image from what you saw in your head. It will look less like a prairie and more like a few scattered fields.

Your calendar app is like a loyal friend watching your back, keeping track of time.

You can make your calendar do amazing tricks by following this simple protocol:

Step 1: Create a timeline.

I encourage you to take the twenty minutes or so to create a timeline on your calendar app. Nail down your prior commitments now, before you address any difficult tasks. Without knowing what time is available for future work sessions, you cannot plan for them accurately.

Step 2: Define your deadline.

Let's assume now that you have your timeline completed, and we'll return to your physics class. You are ready to define your deadline. At your first opportunity, open your calendar app and enter the date and time of the quiz. To make certain it isn't overlooked, select the classification "Highest Priority," which shows up in red. So far, so good.

Step 3: Schedule your sessions.

Next, make a quick evaluation of how long you'll need to study for the quiz. Depending on your present grasp of the material, that estimate will vary, but for the purposes of demonstration, let's say an hour and a half. Once you've got that, you're ready to schedule your sessions. Because physics is a tough subject for many, perhaps you'll want to allow yourself three thirty-minute sessions of study, spread out over the week. If you've prepared your timeline faithfully, you'll be able to see at a glance what your scheduling choices are. Let's imagine 8:00–8:30 p.m. on

Sunday, 7:00–7:30 p.m. on Tuesday, and 8:00–8:30 p.m. on Wednesday, the day before the test. If you follow through by studying during those times, you can feel confident you'll do well on the test. This confidence is evidence of the mastery you are developing over procrastination. Enjoy it!

Step 4: Set alerts.

Of course, when the time for those study sessions rolls around, plenty of new opportunities will arise that could distract you from them. To help you stay on schedule, take a moment to set alerts. I recommend at least two for each session: one ten minutes before each session (to give you time to prepare a workspace and eliminate distractions) and a second to signal the actual start.

While this may sound like an extra step to some of you, setting alerts delivers a lot of bang for your buck. With your calendar app set with functioning alerts, you have, in effect, a loyal friend providing an essential service for you that you cannot do yourself: keeping track of time. When action is required on a task, no matter what else you're engaged in, your app will give you a nudge, reminding you of the task you've decided to own.

Knowing you will get an alert to remind you what you want to get done, and when you want to do it, gives you the freedom to not think about it all the time. Instead of monitoring your calendar every hour or so to see what's coming up, you can relax in the moment, knowing that your calendar app has your back.

Calendar Sharing

If there were such a thing as an extra step in calendar protocol, it would be step 5: *Share your calendar.* I classify it as optional because it's most useful for pleasers. The pleaser's weakness is that you are so unwilling to risk making others unhappy—sometimes even strangers—that you postpone your own needs to please them. When time inevitably runs out, although your social connections are intact, you've failed to maintain another, more important connection. There is literally no time left to connect with yourself.

The calendar app is the go-to tool to counter your tendency to give away the time you need to meet your own needs and goals. When you designate a block of time on your calendar for you, it's a visual reminder that it is *not* to be spent keeping others happy. It's a clear and definite space in time that you have claimed for yourself and are willing to defend. And defend it you must. To illustrate, let's look at how Athena solved one of her difficulties with staying on schedule.

Athena's student council and club meetings, cheerleader practices, and column for the school newspaper take up a lot of time, and her working parents sometimes need help with grocery shopping and driving her brother to swim practice, not to mention her boyfriend, who can be needy. Those activities are all about maintaining Athena's social connections, and when they are accounted for, there's precious little space left on her calendar for what Athena needs to do to take care of herself. If she wants to learn to play the guitar, for example, she knows she'll need to not only plan time for it but also defend that time from the distraction of others' needs and requests.

For the pleaser, setting boundaries that keep loved ones out, however necessary for your own personal happiness, feels rude. You want your friends and family to somehow stay connected with you, even when you're not interacting with them. After all, you're going to need their cooperation for your new attitude to be sustainable. To enlist your friends and family in your new effort to make time for yourself, I recommend the most important tool for the pleaser: the shared calendar.

Don't keep your plans for personal time to yourself. Share them!

Every calendar app gives you the ability to invite others to see, within their own app, whatever events you choose for them to see. For example, when Athena wants an hour every

Wednesday night between 9:00 and 10:00 to watch her favorite TV show, she enters that time block as a repeating event and designates it as part of a shared calendar called *What's up with Athena*. The people most likely to distract her during that time block now have a clear indicator that she has, in effect, invited them *not* to disturb her. They are also, in a subtle way, being included in Athena's plans.

Even those Athena has not invited to her shared calendar can be enlisted to help her take care of herself. If Athena is involved in a group activity, and an alert goes off from her smartphone, when she pulls it out and says, "Guitar practice. Sorry, gotta go!" everybody gets it. Somehow that beeping alert makes her withdrawal from the group feel less to her like she's rejecting them—and less to them like a rejection.

With her hobbies, schoolwork, and relaxation time all nailed down on her shared calendar, Athena is beginning to feel a little more authentic as a person every day. Sometimes her *What's up with Athena* commitments do disappoint others, but Athena is discovering that disappointing others does not necessarily result in getting rejected by them. When others are disappointed by her, they inevitably recover.

Doubling Your Estimate

One of the biggest traps a calendar user can fall into is underestimating how much time you'll need to complete a task. Warriors like Emily, due to their distorted perception of time passing, have difficulty predicting how long they need to complete tasks that aren't engaging.

If Emily guessed that studying for an hour would get her a B on a quiz, she knew from experience that it could wind up taking longer. She could pack a lot of action into an hour of gaming or rock climbing, but studying for tests would feel like swimming in molasses. For warriors, or any type of procrastinator who has difficulty concentrating, I recommend the *Double Your Estimate Rule.* Whatever amount of time you think it will take, *double it.*

For Emily, that meant two hours of studying—*gulp!* She knew she couldn't handle studying that much in one session, so she entered four half-hour study sessions on her calendar. After setting alerts for each, she knew she was prepared and in complete ownership of the task.

When the warrior gets engaged with the calendar app, doubling the time allowed for tasks you need to accomplish, even your most forgettable tasks will get done.

Does maintaining an accurate calendar sound like more work? It is. However, it comes under the category of working smarter, not harder. Leveraging technology empowers you to be more efficient and productive, whatever your pursuit. And nothing is more stressful and time-consuming than scrambling at the last minute to make up for lack of planning. Try using your calendar and see how it works for you!

You can download the directions for using a calendar to help you stay on schedule at http://www.newharbinger .com/35876.

The tools I've introduced thus far are all designed to help you stay focused on the process, not the outcome, of facing challenging tasks. The ideal outcome, of course, is that the task you need to do gets done and you can move forward. But life is seldom that neat, regardless of how well intentioned or hardworking we are. In the next two chapters, we'll look at some of the obstacles that may arise, and how to move forward no matter what happens.

Chapter 15

Coping with Criticism

Athena, as you'll recall, wasn't procrastinating applying for college; she wasn't ready for college and she had other plans for herself. But Athena was putting off something very important—telling her parents.

It wouldn't be easy. Education was an important family value in Athena's household. Both her parents were college graduates, and they had always assumed Athena would get a degree. Once, during dinner, when Athena casually mentioned that one of her friends was forgoing college to play in his band, the shadow that passed over her father's face closed the subject and ruined her appetite for the evening.

Pleasers are particularly sensitive to disapproval or criticism from others, especially those they love. No harsh words need be spoken; all it takes is a look, real or imagined. As a pleaser, if your loved ones aren't happy with you, you worry that your connection with them is at risk. It brings up a primal fear: being rejected by those you depend on and love.

Perfectionists also share this fear of being "kicked out of the tribe," but for a different reason. The perfectionist must feel respected to feel secure, and maintaining that respected status is best done by not making any mistakes, not giving anyone an opportunity to criticize. Jordan believed that getting A's in everything, maintaining a 4.0 GPA, and going to a top college would guarantee him a secure position in society. As long as he performed perfectly, he could never be judged "less than" or not good enough, and he'd always have the respect of others. Or so he thought. Both Athena and Jordan would be well served heeding Eleanor Roosevelt's advice: "Do what you feel in your heart to be right, for you'll be criticized anyway."

*If your loved ones aren't happy with you, it brings up
the primal fear of being rejected, of being alone.*

For the pleaser and the perfectionist, learning to cope with criticism is an essential part of overcoming procrastination. Being sensitive to the judgments of others, you're prone to put off doing anything that may result in those judgments. To get those things done, you'll need to develop some resilience to criticism, which will be especially difficult if, like Jordan and Athena, you've spent your whole life avoiding it. When you've taken ownership of a task that may result in disappointing others, drawing criticism or loss of status, I suggest you try the following exercise.

Exercise: Coping with Criticism

1. Think of something you're afraid of saying or doing because someone might criticize you.

2. Imagine the worst thing that person might say or think about you if you did this thing.

3. Think up an assertive response. (Assertiveness is standing up for yourself, not putting others down.) What are you afraid that person might say to your assertive response? Answer that with another assertive response.

4. Continue coming up with assertive responses to everything you are afraid that person might think or say.

To download a *Coping With Criticism* worksheet, go to http://www.newharbinger.com/35876.

With this practice, remember that all you're doing is practicing standing up for yourself while tolerating others' disagreement or criticism. *Don't fall into the trap of trying to convince them that you are right or to make them see it your way.* The point is not to get others on your side. It's to get *you* on your side!

Here is Athena's completed coping practice for her task of telling her parents her plans for a gap year:

Parents: We know better than you what's good for you, and if you really cared about us, you wouldn't do this.

Athena: You may know better what is good for me and you might be right, but part of me growing up is doing what I believe is right. Even if I'm wrong, I can learn from this.

Parents: You're foolish and a terrible disappointment to us. This will ruin your life.

Athena: I'm sorry you think that, and it's hard for me to do this without your support, but this is part of me growing up.

Parents: Well, if you want to ruin your life, go ahead!

Athena: I'm not trying to ruin my life. I'm learning to stand up for what I want to do.

Parents: This is the worst decision you've ever made!

Athena: I know you don't think this is what I should be doing, but it takes courage for me to do what I think is best for me and not to rely only on what you think. This is part of growing up.

You can turbocharge your coping practice by asking a trusted friend to play the role of the person you fear will criticize you. If you cannot find someone to practice with, write your own script, then read it aloud. When you hear the critical words spoken, you get a more powerful experience of what you are afraid someone might say. And saying your assertive responses out loud will empower you in a way that imagining them cannot.

If you have any trouble coming up with assertive responses, review chapter 9 for help. And if you find your passion fading, remind yourself of the personal values you are moving toward: (1) acting instead of procrastinating, (2) standing up for yourself, and most important, (3) achieving deeper, more meaningful personal connections with others by being authentic.

Whether to achieve excellence or authentic social connections, we must develop resilience regarding the judgments of others.

Although Jordan's coping practice may look and sound quite a bit different, at the heart of it, the perfectionist's challenge is the same as the pleaser's. To take the risks necessary to achieve the excellence the perfectionist desires, you must have resilience regarding the judgments of others about your mistakes. In other words, the perfectionist must be comfortable with mistakes. Does this mean you need to be happy with the mistake itself? No. It means you won't let mistakes get in the way of your happiness.

This will take practice, and a great place to start is to imagine yourself falling short at something important to you, like getting a lower grade on a test than you expect, making an error on the sports field, or saying something in a group of people that isn't well received. When you have the situation in your mind, imagine the worst possible thing that others might think about you, and what an assertive response might be. Here's some dialogue from Jordan's coping practice based on his fear of being judged or criticized if he should do poorly on his SATs. Remember, coping practice dialogue is not based on what people will actually think or say, but rather on what you are most *afraid* they will think or say.

Teacher: I'm really disappointed in you, Jordan. You had so much potential. I expected more of you.

Jordan: I understand that you're disappointed. I am, too. But I can learn from my mistakes.

Teacher: This mistake indicates that you don't deserve to get into a good college.

Jordan: It's possible that this will affect what colleges will accept me, but I did the best I could. I did well at some things and less well at others.

Teacher: Well, the best you could is not good enough! You've lost my respect.

Jordan: I'm sorry that I've lost your respect, but I know that my performance doesn't make me a less worthy person. Trying and making mistakes is better than not trying at all, and I did try.

Note that Jordan's assertions, like Athena's, were less about convincing others and more about convincing himself. Coping practice is designed to remind you who you are at a time when you are most vulnerable to forgetting, when you are afraid of being judged by others. For the perfectionist, "who you are" is someone who values excellence and

Coping practice is designed to remind you who you are at a time when you are most vulnerable to forgetting, when you are afraid of being judged by others.

is willing to risk failure—and losing others' respect—to achieve it.

Coping with criticism is a valuable practice for every teen, including warriors and rebels. When Emily's friends tease her about her messy room, she feels ashamed. And as everyone who's been shamed knows, it isn't likely to change our behavior. Shame is a kind of stress, and when Emily is stressed, the last thing she'll do is embrace a boring task like housework. She'll get lost in a game or something else that engages her. To change any behavior, we need to be motivated from within ourselves, not from without.

And while Tyler, as a rebel, may seem like someone who doesn't care what others think, the exact opposite can be true. Rebels want to be different from everybody else, but not because they want to be alone. If you're a rebel, you want to stand out as unique *within your social group*. You want others in your group to value you as in some way different and special. The worst criticism Tyler can imagine is being viewed as one of the crowd. For example, Tyler bought a new jacket that he thought he looked great in, but when he got to school the next day, he noticed three other students with the same jacket. That evening he was back at the mall returning it. Tyler wanted to stand out, not to blend in.

The more you practice with worst-case scenarios where you are being judged, criticized, even mocked, the more accustomed you'll be to the negative waves of emotion that arise, and the better able to ride them. Greet them with a deep, diaphragmatic breath, and remind yourself who you are and the values you are working toward. In addition to the values of excellence, connection, engagement, and autonomy, here are some more you can employ.

honesty	creativity
courage	risk
purpose	autonomy
growth	fun
kindness	pleasure
commitment	responsibility

At this point, I've introduced all the tools you need to take control of the tasks you've been procrastinating on. If you can identify unhelpful underlying beliefs, let new beliefs take root, breathe and ride the wave, divide until doable, eliminate distractions, beat the clock, stay on schedule, and cope with criticism, you are going to be one badass taskmaster.

But even if you are successful with all these tools, there's one obstacle remaining that can thwart your best efforts at overcoming procrastination. That obstacle is your own natural tendency to protect yourself from the vulnerability of your type. In the next chapter, I'll define the last challenge for every procrastinator: knowing what it is that you are—and aren't—aiming for.

When you are resilient to criticism, you can get the things done that you need to get done, whether others like it or not!

Chapter 16

Hitting the Target, Not the Bull's-Eye

Remember Robin Hood? After his opponent hit a bull's-eye, the legendary archer drew back his bow and let his arrow fly, splitting his opponent's arrow down the center. A bull's-eye on top of a bull's-eye; if only life were that glorious and simple!

Whether you're a serious archer or a casual dart thrower, you know that hitting the bull's-eye is the exception, not the rule. Although we aim for it every time, we seldom shoot straight enough to hit the exact center, and when we do, we shout with surprise and joy. So why, when we take on a task in our everyday lives, do we grade ourselves on whether we hit the bull's-eye?

Major league baseball fans certainly don't judge players' performance that way. When a star home-run hitter steps up to the plate, eleven times out of twelve, he *fails to hit a home run*! Two times out of three, he fails to even get a hit. Nobody categorizes singles, doubles, triples, walks, and strikeouts as "not-home-runs." Coaches judge players on whether they're using the correct batting stance, making a smooth swing, and being patient and not swinging at bad pitches. Batters know that if they approach the plate following rules they have practiced, they are more likely be productive, which includes possibly hitting homers.

The tasks we put off are almost always those where we're afraid we'll miss the bull's-eye. To the perfectionist, a bull's-eye means getting it perfect, without a mistake. The pleaser's bull's-eye is making everyone happy. The warrior's is not being bored and feeling fully engaged. And for the rebel, the dead center of the target is feeling independent.

All the tools in this book won't help you if you are still thinking that you need to hit your bull's-eye. The fact is, no matter how much determination, commitment, and preparation you can muster for a task, if it has challenged you in the past, your arrow is not likely to land dead center. You're going to need to change your idea of what success means.

When it isn't necessary to hit the bull's-eye, all things are possible.

When practicing piano you hit a lot of wrong notes. In batting practice you often swing and miss. Target practice is the same. When your arrow lands outside the bull's-eye, that's okay.

Your job with any task you've decided to own is simply to get on with it. That's why I advise my clients to *Hit the target, not the bull's-eye.* Without the pressure of a perfect outcome, starting the task will be less formidable, and your chances of completing it will be greater.

Target practice is especially important for perfectionists and pleasers, who have strong attachments to their bull's-eyes. Perfectionist Jordan's bull's-eye was getting an "A"; his passion for excellence demanded nothing less. But since he was unsure and confused about what to write for his essay, and he didn't feel clear headed, a perfect grade seemed unlikely. The illustration below shows what Jordan felt like after his first essay writing session: nothing but misses.

What happens when you take your focus off the bull's-eye and look at the whole target? Here's what changed for Jordan.

RISK MAKING MISTAKES

USE 5-MIN JUMP START

DIVIDE UNTIL DOABLE

Of course, Jordan might still get an A. But his job is merely to stay on the target. The only way he could miss this target would be to delay action; that is, to procrastinate. If you believe that as long as you are hitting the target you are doing well, you're much less likely to put off the task. Expanding your attention beyond the bull's-eye to the whole target, you'll evaluate your work more favorably, which will help you tackle the task next time.

As a pleaser, Athena's bull's-eye was not disappointing anyone she loved, and thinking she had to hit it was making her put off a task that sooner or later she had to complete. How could Athena break this news to her parents about her gap-year plans without upsetting and disappointing them?

Was there a way that would make it easier on them?

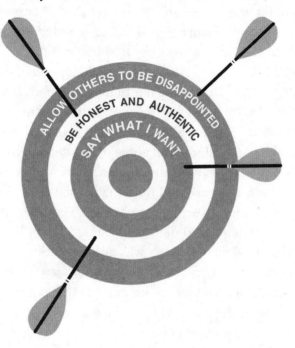

Athena's procrastination was about more than disappointing her parents. They could get angry with her. As a pleaser, Athena's core value—social connection—was at risk. To accomplish this task, Athena had to widen her aim beyond the "keep her parents happy" bull's-eye and see the whole target. Here's Athena's target after she met with them and told them her plan.

Once Athena identified her real goals, the task became much more doable. She didn't have to hit the bull's-eye of pleasing her parents anymore. Success for her was to stay on the target.

But it wasn't easy for Athena to see how well she'd done. Athena's habit was to feel guilty and get mad at herself whenever she disappointed anyone, and that was her first instinct this time, too.

If you believe that as long as you are hitting the target you are doing well, you're much less likely to put off the task.

Although Athena's parents weren't as upset by her plan as she had imagined, they had a lot of counterarguments they wanted her to listen to, and they grilled her about some of the details, like where she would live and how she would support herself. They seemed hurt that Athena had waited so long to tell them, which, of course, was very painful for a pleaser like Athena. She'd definitely missed the bull's-eye.

And that was okay! Athena was authentic. She risked upsetting them. She explained her point of view without hedging anything. And when her parents did express some disappointment, she didn't try to take care of them in any of her old ways. She just rode the wave.

Athena was definitely on the target. I encouraged her to give herself a pat on the back for what she'd done right. And I told her what I often tell my clients: a pat on the back for hitting the target makes a lot more sense than a kick in the butt for missing the bull's-eye!

"Hitting the target, not the bull's-eye" is most essential for the perfectionist and the pleaser because they both tend to judge themselves harshly. But the other two types of procrastinators can also benefit by adjusting what they are aiming at.

Emily's bull's-eye is full engagement. Unless she feels stimulated enough to feel completely absorbed in the task—physically, mentally, or both—she feels bored, dull, and useless. Of course, every time a warrior completes a boring task—or even the smallest doable part of a boring task—it *is* an accomplishment. Staying on task despite being bored is the hardest thing for the warrior to do. But if you are preoccupied with what didn't happen—feeling engaged and focused, with mental and physical reflexes firing effortlessly—you're likely to overlook what you've accomplished and skip the celebration you deserve. In the following illustration, we envision Emily's target when cleaning her room.

Can you create full engagement doing tasks that bore the heck out of you? Probably not. What you can do is identify the target that goes with the task, and reward yourself for hitting it. The reward can be literal, as in allowing yourself specific time playing a video game or watching a movie, or it can be psychological, as in reviewing how accomplishing the task brings you closer to a personal goal that will fully engage you.

Your reward can even be whimsical. If you envision your target like a dartboard, giving each concentric ring a value, you can keep score. Whatever your method of rewarding yourself, don't be faint with the praise. Remember that for you, battling boredom is the biggest battle of all. Winning that battle is what makes a hero out of a warrior.

The rebel's bull's-eye is independence, doing tasks that are your idea to do. But as a rebel, you'll be faced with lots of tasks assigned or inspired by others that don't make sense to you. If you need to hit the independence bull's-eye, you'll postpone those tasks as long as you can get away with it.

By opening up the entire target, you'll make the tasks you need to get done to advance your overall independence much more rewarding. Here's what Tyler's default target might look like for any task that challenges his short-term independence.

When we conceptualize a challenging task, or any doable part of a challenging task, as a target rather than a bull's-eye, we allow ourselves more ways to win. Winning creates more motivation for us to meet future challenging tasks head-on, rather than putting them off.

Exercise: Hit the Target

Identify your bull's-eye. Write it down so you have a visual reminder of what you're *not* needing to accomplish with this task.

Ask yourself, *What does "being on the target" mean for this task?* Write down the specific things you come up with on your target. Using any of the tools in this book would be on the target. For example, letting a new belief take root can be a ring on the target. Other rings might be choosing a time for a five-minute jump-start, riding a wave of negative emotion while doing a task, dividing the task until it's doable, and eliminating distractions.

You can download a blank *Hit the Target* worksheet at http://www.newharbinger.com/35876.

To cultivate more of this motivation—what might be called a winning attitude—reward yourself every time you hit the target, no matter how insignificant it may be. When, rather than catering to her boyfriend's need to hang out after school, Athena chooses to practice guitar, she wins. She missed her "Keep everyone happy" bull's-eye, but she's on the target when she takes care of her own needs.

When Jordan gets his history essay back with a correction circled in red and an A-, he's missed his "It has to be perfect" bull's-eye. But he still wins because his target includes "risk making mistakes." Emily may feel bored out of her mind while doing her laundry—no bull's-eye for her—but she did think to double the time she allotted for the chore, and ride the wave when she got bored. That's being on the target.

Every time you hit the target is a cause for celebration. Be generous to yourself and, no matter how insignificant what you've done may seem, lavish the praise. Every time you complete a doable, you can either pat yourself on the back for being on target or kick yourself in the butt for missing the bull's-eye. The choice is yours!

It's quite possible, perhaps even likely, that when you opened this book you were tempted to put off reading it. Getting this far may have involved numerous battles with the procrastination beast and, if so, I want to offer you my congratulations! Reading any book that challenges the way you think and behave is difficult. The fact that you did it is

praiseworthy. I hope you give yourself a pat on the back, or the equivalent, to acknowledge your curiosity, honesty, and persistence.

In the final chapter I'll try to give you a little perspective of what is at stake for you, and a few words that I hope will inspire you. Like the other chapters, it's short—a doable for sure.

Chapter 17

Conclusion

Procrastination is widely perceived as something teens do, but you don't have to look far to see evidence that most adults have a problem with putting off challenging tasks as well. When we repeatedly use procrastination as a way of avoiding problem tasks, we create well-worn neurological pathways in the brain that are difficult to break. Tasks that challenge our needs to be perfect, to be socially connected, to feel fully engaged, or to feel independent can form a kind of ceiling over our lives, a barrier we cannot move beyond. You can spend a lifetime devising ways to avoid having your core values challenged.

For those cherished core values to become fully realized, they need to be tested. For you to become truly excellent in your field of endeavor, you'll need to take risks and make mistakes. To live a life of full engagement, you'll have to manage tedium and time. To enjoy deep and meaningful relationships, your authenticity will inevitably disappoint others at times, and to achieve a sustainable independence, you'll have to cooperate with others even when it makes little sense to you.

The good news is that whatever your values and whatever your dreams for the future may be, there is no better time to begin making them real than right now. Your teenage brain is supple and more amenable to new learning and experience than it will be at any other period of your life. Your reading this book gives evidence of your curiosity and willingness to ask hard questions, as well as explore new answers. These qualities will help you master not only procrastination but also every challenge that lies ahead.

For the perfectionist, learning to tolerate making mistakes will enable you to be more daring and creative in everything you do. Accepting and rewarding yourself for being on the target will give you the encouragement you need to strive for even bigger and better things in life. Focusing on the doable part of the task at hand instead of the end results will allow you to live more fully in the present and will decrease your overall stress and anxiety level. Freed from the constraint of perfection, the excellence you value most will manifest naturally.

Perfectionist: Focusing on the doable part of the task instead of the end results will allow you to live more fully in the present and will decrease your stress and anxiety.

For the warrior, learning how to tolerate boredom and tedium will help you reach the more fully engaging levels where you will thrive. Using calendars and reminders will help you compensate for the different way you perceive the passage of time, liberating you from the shame you may experience by being out of sync with those around you and by your tendency to be late to things. When you learn to engage with tasks that don't engage you, great things are possible.

Warrior: Learning how to tolerate boredom and tedium will help you reach the more fully engaging levels where you will thrive.

For the pleaser, learning to stand up for yourself will help you be more honest and authentic in your relationships with others. Blocking out and defending the time you need for yourself will discourage others from taking you for granted. When you disappoint others, you'll become increasingly better at riding the wave of fear of losing your connection with them. And because you won't be draining your own resources to meet their needs, you'll have more energy to give when it's needed.

> **Pleaser:** Completing tasks that help you take care of
> yourself will help you be more authentic and connected in
> your relationships with others.

As a rebel, learning to own tasks that serve you—even
when they're assigned or inspired by others—will move you
closer to the independence and autonomy that is so important
to you. By asking yourself whether doing the task serves your
long-term interests, you're taking charge of your own life and
your future. Creating your own timeline to accomplish an
assigned task puts you in charge. With these skills, should you
choose, you can morph from a rebel into a leader.

> **Rebel:** By determining whether doing a task serves your
> long-term interests, you're taking charge of your own life
> and your future.

Whatever your type, when you use technology as a tool
for, rather than a distraction from, getting things done, you're
mastering a challenge previous generations did not have to
deal with.

And remember that when you hit the target, not the bull's-
eye, you open up a world of ways to win. Give yourself praise
for the work you did, instead of a kick in the pants for what
you did not do. The more you're rewarded for being on target,
the more your motivation and self-esteem will grow. There

are no limits to what you can do when you're free from the tyranny of the bull's-eye.

But perhaps most important, your practice riding the waves of negative emotion that accompany challenging tasks will build resilience to the pain that drives the cycle of procrastination. Tolerating, indeed welcoming, negative emotion is the key to breaking that cycle. Just as a beginning skydiver learns to leap out of the plane despite fear, you'll learn to leap toward any task that is necessary for your personal progress, no matter how painful it may appear to be.

Before I close, I have some questions for you. Did Jordan, Emily, Athena, or Tyler strike you as lazy? Were any of them weak? How about stupid? I hope that, if nothing else, you've learned from this book that procrastination is not a mark of shame. It's a human problem that has a solution. If it's a problem for you, the tools to solve it are here. Once you start to use them, you'll find yourself getting things done. But more important, you'll find yourself getting what you wanted in your heart all along: excellence, engagement, connection, and independence.

Jennifer Shannon, LMFT, is author of *The Shyness and Social Anxiety Workbook for Teens*, *The Anxiety Survival Guide for Teens*, and *Don't Feed the Monkey Mind*. She is in private practice in Santa Rosa, CA, and is a diplomate of the Academy of Cognitive Therapy.

Doug Shannon is a freelance cartoonist.

More ⏱Instant Help Books for Teens

An Imprint of New Harbinger Publications

OVERCOMING PROCRASTINATION FOR TEENS
A CBT Guide for College-Bound Students
ISBN: 978-1626254572 / US $16.95

GET OUT OF YOUR MIND & INTO YOUR LIFE FOR TEENS
A Guide to Living an Extraordinary Life
ISBN: 978-1608821938 / US $15.95

THE PERFECTIONISM WORKBOOK FOR TEENS
Activities to Help You Reduce Anxiety & Get Things Done
ISBN: 978-1626254541 / US $16.95

THE SELF-ESTEEM WORKBOOK FOR TEENS
Activities to Help You Build Confidence & Achieve Your Goals
ISBN: 978-1608825820 / US $15.95

THE MINDFUL TEEN
Powerful Skills to Help You Handle Stress One Moment at a Time
ISBN: 978-1626250802 / US $17.95

THE GRIT GUIDE FOR TEENS
A Workbook to Help You Build Perseverance, Self-Control & a Growth Mindset
ISBN: 978-1626258563 / US $16.95

Register your **new harbinger** titles for additional benefits!

When you register your **new harbinger** title—purchased in any format, from any source—you get access to benefits like the following:

- Downloadable accessories like printable worksheets and extra content

- Instructional videos and audio files

- Information about updates, corrections, and new editions

Not every title has accessories, but we're adding new material all the time.

Access free accessories in 3 easy steps:

1. Sign in at NewHarbinger.com (or **register** to create an account).

2. Click on **register a book**. Search for your title and click the **register** button when it appears.

3. Click on the **book cover or title** to go to its details page. Click on **accessories** to view and access files.

That's all there is to it!

If you need help, visit:

NewHarbinger.com/accessories

new harbinger
CELEBRATING
40 YEARS